How to Receive from God

How to Receive from God

10 Steps to Living in Victory

by
Tom Brown

Tom Brown Ministries
El Paso, Texas

HOW TO RECEIVE FROM GOD

ISBN 0-9658305-2-7

published by
Tom Brown Ministries
P.O. Box 27275
El Paso, Texas 79926
(915) 857-0962
Email: tom@tbm.org
Internet: www.tbm.org

Unless other wise indicated, all Scripture quotations are taken from the Holy Bible, *New International Version* (NIV), copyright 1973, 1978, 1984 by the International Bible Society. Used by permission.

Scripture quotations marked (Ways) are from the *Ways Translation* of the Holy Bible. Published by McMillan and Company Limited (1935 Seventh Edition).

Scripture quotations marked (KJV) are from the *King James Version* of the Bible.

Scripture quotations marked (Living) are from *The Living Bible*, copyright 1971 by Tyndale House Publishers. Used by permission.

Scripture quotations marked (TCNT) are from the *Twentieth Century New Testament* published by Fleming H. Revell Company (1904).

Scripture quotations marked (Amp) are from *The Amplified Bible*, copyright 1987 by the Zondervan Corporation and the Lockman Foundation. Used by permission

Contents

Preface

Now faith is the substance of things hoped for, the evidence of things not seen. For by it the elders obtained a good report. Through faith we understand that the worlds were framed by the word of God, so that things which are seen were not made of things which do appear. – (Hebrews 11:1-3, KJV)

Faith is an untapped minefield wherein lies the riches of God's grace. Although this passage has been used more often than any other text, people have only begun to dig the surface of these rich scriptures. This book, hopefully, will make a contribution just as the Rockefellers did with oil. The oil had always been there. Many tried to tap the oil, but the Rockefellers did it with more success. I think this book has successfully dug into the riches of faith.

Why another book on faith? Well, if this book were simply a rehashing of what has already been taught, then I would not have thought it worthwhile to write it. It is my humble, heartfelt conviction that this book presents some very new and profound revelations on faith.

You will find yourself rejoicing and weeping, as you discover the riches that God has planned for you. All it takes is faith. Sounds simple. It is, yet at the same time, it is not. There is so much to learn about faith, and now you will attend the school of faith, so you can say with Paul, "I have learned in whatsoever condition I am to be independent of circumstances. I am schooled to bear the deepness of poverty; I am schooled to bear abundance. In life as a whole and in all its circumstances I have mastered the secret of living — how to be the same amidst repletion and starvation, amidst abundance and privation. I am equal to every lot through the help of Him Who gives me inward strength" (Phil 4:11-13, Ways Translation). It is time for you to say, "**I have mastered the secret of living.**"

Faith is the way to master living. When you have neared mastery, you will be at a place where impossibilities turn to possibilities, where sickness turns to health, and where poverty turns to wealth. Come on! Let's dig together and mine the riches of God's abundant wealth.

Introduction

Susan had fond memories of being bussed to church when she was ten. She loved Sunday school, loved the teachers and felt peace at church. Later as she grew up, she got mixed up with the wrong crowd. She smoked, drank and became promiscuous.

Feeling empty after two troubled marriages, she finally went back to church, desperately wanting peace again.

Yet as much as she tried, she couldn't feel it. She felt God had abandoned her because of her sinful ways.

The minister had counseled her and led her in the sinner's prayer, but still she did not feel forgiven. She feared going to hell.

One day as Susan was watching a television special, she saw a minister who was used in deliverance. At that moment, she knew that demons were the cause of her troubles. Eventually she found a way to attend one of his meetings. When she got there, she felt the power of God in a way she never had before. The minister had a unique boldness as he told the congregation that there was someone who needed deliverance. Susan wept while he spoke because she felt like he was speaking to her. She then rushed forward for prayer, and while the minister commanded the demons to leave she heard a strange voice speaking through her, "She's mine. I'm not going to leave!" The minister was undaunted, he boldly told the devil that she has been forgiven and cleansed by the blood of Jesus. In minutes she was free.

Susan felt better than she ever had. For months she continued to walk closely with the Lord.

One day, however, someone told her about the unforgivable sin of blasphemy against the Spirit. The thought struck her that she might have committed this sin. After thinking about this possibility, she began to feel nervous. She began to feel empty again as her fears turned to depression. Eventually she became sure that she had committed this sin and believed that God would not forgive her.

After this she still attended church, and every time the minister would give the altar call, she would either go forward or wanted to go forward, but still she felt nothing. She couldn't receive the assurance of her salvation and forgiveness of sins. She eventually went back to drinking and sleeping around.

She plunged deeper into despair. She even attempted suicide twice. For the last few years she has been in and out of mental hospitals. Ministers have talked to her, but she continues to believe that God will not forgive her.

BOB GREW UP WITHOUT CHURCH, yet the curiosity of a city-wide crusade conducted by a famous evangelist led him to attend one in his city. As he heard the Reverend speak, tears welled up in his eyes. He couldn't believe what he was feeling.

When the altar call was given, he found himself running forward to be saved. He experienced a glorious salvation.

He immediately attended one of the recommended churches and quickly became a Sunday school teacher. He loved the Word!

Bob was a full-fledged disciple of Christ, but was disappointed with many of the members in his church. They didn't seem as enthusiastic as he. So you can imagine his excitement when he met some Christians who were hungry for God just like him. They were from another church, a Pentecostal church.

Bob had heard something about them, but was discouraged from going to "those kind" of churches. Despite warnings, he decided to attend, and quickly he was convinced that there was something special about the church. It seemed that everyone was thrilled about Christ. When he asked the pastor what the difference was between this church and his own, the pastor said it was the baptism in the Holy Spirit.

What!? Bob had just taught about the baptism in the Spirit. It was part of the Sunday school quarterly that he used for his lessons. The denominational quarterly said that salvation was the same as the baptism in the Holy Spirit, but now the Pentecostal pastor explained the difference. He also told Bob that he would speak in tongues when he received this experience.

Bob thanked the pastor but wasn't ready for such a thing. He told a few friends at his church what the pastor had said about the baptism in the Spirit. The friends squealed on him and told the pastor. The pastor was quite concerned about Bob "falling for the Pentecostal experience". He talked with him and explained the denominational view on the baptism in the Spirit. Bob seemed convinced, but why were those Pentecostals so exuberant? Maybe there was something to that experience.

Bob snuck back to the Pentecostal church during a special revival service. The evangelist taught about the Baptism in the Spirit and speaking in tongues. Bob decided to give this experience a chance. He came forward and the evangelists laid his hands on Bob, but he felt nothing. No tongues. No feelings. Nothing like he remembered at the large crusade. Bob concluded that tongues were not for him.

He went back to his church where he continues to serve to this day, though his enthusiasm seems to be waning.

HARRIET, A DEVOUT MEMBER IN HER CHURCH, has been in and out of hospitals for as long as she can remember. She believes that God can and does heal, but she has not experienced it herself. Everyone in her church knows her condition. She has made it plain to everyone.

A few believers have offered to pray for her. She doesn't overtly turn down their prayers, but she does remind them of certain "crosses" they must all bear. She lets the prayer warriors know that although she suffers, she puts up with it patiently. After making it clear to them that her illness might be for God's glory, she then allows prayer. She makes sure to end every prayer with...

"If it is God's Will."

Although she knows God can cure, she does question those who claim to have the gifts to do it. She *has* allowed the elders of the church to pray over her with oil, because she knows it's mentioned in James 5:15 to let the elders pray for healing, but she is skeptical of "faith healers."

Nevertheless, when a famous healing evangelist came to town, she was willing to give him a chance. The crusade was full of excitement, she admitted, but she wondered if all those people who claimed to have been healed that night were *really* healed.

During the meeting, she asked God to heal her. She insisted, "Lord, I don't doubt that you can heal, and you know it has been a long time since I have lived without pain, so I ask you to heal me tonight. I want you to get all the glory so do it sovereignly, without hands being laid on me. I don't want others claiming they healed me." She shed a few tears waiting for the possibility that the Lord heard her humble plea, but nothing happened.

She hobbled out the huge auditorium still bound with her sickness — carrying "her cross". To this day, she tells you that she believes in healing, and is waiting patiently for the Lord to heal her, or take her home to heaven if it is His will.

PASTOR HANK IS KNOWN FOR HIS MISSIONARY ZEAL and compassion for his flock. That hasn't seemed to be enough to grow his ministry, however. Fresh out of seminary, he was full of zeal but ever since he took the pastorate of his first church, he has struggled financially. He has worked hard to add people to the church, and the church has grown somewhat, but with more people comes more bills, and he just can't seem to make it.

He has heard of a couple of pastors in his city that are doing great financially. They started small like him, but with their television ministries going strong they have grown tremendously.

Pastor Hank knows if he could afford it, he too would go on TV, but there isn't money in the budget for it. Why can't the church prosper?

Several years have passed and his children have grown up. Now he has to help with college expenses. For the first time, he has seriously considered resigning and getting a secular job that could adequately provide for his family. He feels like a failure.

He knows passages like Philippians 4:19, but it doesn't seem to be working for him. His needs are not really being met like they should. He knows his church needs to be more generous, but he doesn't want to look greedy by teaching too much on giving. Besides, he believes people should give out of love — not expecting God to bless them. He just does not believe in "tithing" like some churches although he admits those churches are prospering.

Failed to Receive from God

These people, though the names are fictional, are compilations of real people that have one thing in common: they did not receive from God what He had promised. They were all sincere, much like the Old Testament saints: *These were all commended for their faith, yet none of them received what had been*

14

promised (Heb 11:39).

For us under the New Covenant it is not necessary to fail to receive from God. *God had planned something better for us so that only together with us would they be made perfect* (Heb 11:40).

Rather than feel that it is our lot in life to go without God's promised blessings, we should expect more under the New Covenant, because *God had planned something better for us.* The *something better* includes receiving from God all He has planned for us — assurance of salvation, baptism in the Spirit, health for our bodies, needed prosperity and a host of other blessings.

There are other blessings that God has promised: answered prayer, moving mountains, deliverance from demons, restoration of marriages, success in ministry, freedom from addictions, and so much more.

If you have struggled with receiving from God, then this book is for you. Or perhaps you have been praying for someone, and yet, they have not been able to receive from God. This book will help provide answers to you too.

Step One:
KNOW WHAT GOD HAS PROMISED

he righteous will live by his faith (HAB 2:4).
Simple statement, but the ramifications are
far reaching. This passage is so powerful
that the apostle Paul quoted it three times in his
epistles (see Rom 1:17, Gal 3:11 and Heb 10:38).

He doesn't simply say the sinner is saved by
faith, or the sick is healed by faith. No! He says the
righteous will *live by his faith*. The phrase to "live
by" means to survive, subsist, maintain, live, and
acquire a livelihood. There is not a stronger
English phrase to emphasize the absolute essential
need of something. Food, water and air are essential and we physically live by them. This means
there is not an element, situation or area in which
faith is irrelevant.

For in the gospel a righteousness from God is
revealed, a righteousness *that is by faith from first to
last* (Rom 1:17). Faith is the *beginning* and *ending* of
the Christian life. We started off with faith, and we
should end in faith. Of course, faith does not end,
because our relationship with God is eternal. Faith,
along with hope and love will continue throughout eternity. There will never be a moment when
faith is unnecessary or obsolete.

You cannot have any sort of relationship with God apart from faith. *And without faith it is impossible to please God, because anyone who comes to him must believe that he exists and that he rewards those who earnestly seek him* (Heb 11:6). The most important duty of man is *to please God*. The scripture makes it clear, you cannot please God without faith. Faith must be your primary aim. The benefits of faith are clear: *God rewards those who earnestly seek him.*

You cannot become the person you want to be, or achieve your God-given potential, or receive anything from God without faith. *He who doubts is like a wave of the sea, blown and tossed by the wind. That man should not think he will receive anything from the Lord* (James 1:6-7). Faith is so vital and important that a person who does not believe God should not even think he could receive *anything* from the Lord. *Anything* covers everything.

The Blessings of Faith

Consider these many passages that show the importance of faith.

1. We are saved by faith.

Ephesians 2:8: *For it is by grace you have been saved, through faith.*

2. We are justified by faith.

Romans 5:1: *Therefore, since we have been justified through faith, we have peace with God through our Lord Jesus Christ.*

3. We have access into grace by faith.

Romans 5:2: *through whom we have gained access by faith into this grace in which we now stand.*

4. We are protected by faith.

1 Peter 1:5: *who through faith are shielded by God's power until the coming of the salvation that is ready to be revealed in the last time.*

5. We are blessed by faith.

Galatians 3:9: *So those who have faith are blessed along with Abraham, the man of faith.*

6. We receive the Spirit by faith.

Galatians 3:14: *He redeemed us in order that the blessing given to Abraham might come to the Gentiles through Christ Jesus, so that by faith we might receive the promise of the Spirit.*

7. We are sanctified by faith.

Acts 26:18: *so that they may receive forgiveness of sins and a place among those who are sanctified by faith in me.*

8. We inherit the promises by faith.

Hebrews 6:12: *We do not want you to become lazy, but to imitate those who through faith and patience inherit what has been promised.*

9. We resist Satan by faith.

1 Peter 5:9: *Resist [Satan], standing firm in the faith.*

10. We overcome the world by faith.

1 John 5:4: *for everyone born of God overcomes the world. This is the victory that has overcome the world, even our faith.*

11. We receive answers to prayers by faith.

Matthew 21:22: *If you believe, you will receive whatever you ask for in prayer.*

12. We receive wisdom by faith.

James 1:5,6: *If any of you lacks wisdom, he should ask God, who gives generously to all without finding fault, and it will be given to him. But when he asks, he must believe and not doubt.*

13. We are healed by faith.

Matthew 9:22: *Jesus turned and saw her. "Take heart, daughter," he said, "your faith has healed you." And the woman was healed from that moment.*

14. We receive the supply of material needs by faith.

Matthew 6:30: *If that is how God clothes the grass of the field, which is here today and tomorrow is thrown into the fire, will he not much more clothe you, O you of little faith.*

15. We move mountains of difficulties by faith.

Matthew 17:20: *if you have faith as small as a mustard seed, you can say to this mountain, 'Move from here to there' and it will move. Nothing will be impossible to you.*

It is clear that *everything* we receive and *everything* we can do and *everything* we can become is a result of faith. Many have failed to receive all God has for them because they lacked faith.

The problem with receiving from God has nothing to do with whether or not God is giving, but whether or not we have been receiving.

Four truths about God's nature to Give

Look at what James says: *If any of you lacks wisdom, he should ask God, who gives generously to all without finding fault, and it will be given to him. But when he asks, he must believe and not doubt, because he who doubts is like a wave of the sea, blown and tossed by the wind. That man should not think he will receive anything from the Lord; he is a double-minded man, unstable in all he does* (James 1:5-8).

The man *who doubts should not think he will receive anything from the Lord.* The problem is **not** that God has failed to give to the man, but the doubting man has failed to *receive* what God is giving. Yet many excuse their failure to receive by claiming that God did not give to them. Someone who does not get healed may say that God did not heal them. In other words, they blame God for not healing, instead of them not receiving the health He is giving.

It is obvious that before one can receive, God must give. Giving always precedes receiving. Here in this passage, James gives us four momentous truths about God's nature to give. God by nature is a giver. God is love, and love gives.

1. God continually gives.

James says, "*If any of you lacks wisdom, he should ask God, who gives...*" There is no question whether or not God will give. God is one *who gives*. He does not know any other way. The word *gives* in this passage is a verb tense that we do not have in English. We have only past, present and future tenses. In the Greek language there is a continual, present tense verb. Greek scholar, Mr. Strongs calls this Greek word "a prolonged form of a primary verb." Acts 6:4 says, "*will give...continually*" (KJV). That describes this word. God *gives continually*. He doesn't begin to give; He was already giving before you asked. That is why God says, "Before you called I answered." God already provided the answer before you asked.

God gives twenty-four hours a day, seven days a week, three hundred and sixty-five days a year and one extra for leap year. He is always giving. Before you could ask Him to heal you, He already gave you healing.

This is what Peter understood when he prayed for Aeneas: *As Peter traveled about the country, he went to visit the saints in Lydda. There he found a man named Aeneas, a paralytic who had been bedridden for eight years. "Aeneas," Peter said to him, "Jesus Christ heals you. Get up and take care of your mat." Immediately Aeneas got up* (Acts 9:32-34).

Peter did not say, "Aeneas, Jesus will heal you." That would have made Jesus healing in the future. No! Peter says, *"Jesus Christ heals you."* Peter was saying, "Jesus is healing you now! He was always healing you, Aeneas, even though you have been bedridden for eight years. He was healing you eight years ago. So get up and take care of your mat. Act like he has always been healing you."

Prayer does not make God give. God was giving before you could pray. He was giving you wisdom before you asked Him for it. He was giving you the money, before you could mention the need to Him. He was taking care of your problems before you could pray for help. God is always giving.

2. God gives generously.

The second truth James mentions about God's nature to give is *God, who gives generously.* God is not a cheapskate. He does not give just enough. As Jesse Duplantis likes to say, "God is too much!" He is called in the Hebrew, "El Shaddai." He is not *El Cheapo*! *El Shaddai* means *more than enough*.

Paul describes God's abundant ability and super generosity in this way: *Now to him who is able to do immeasurably more than all we ask or imagine, according to his power that is at work within us* (Eph 3:20).

We can never ask for more than what God has to give. We don't ask for a Cadillac and God says, "I'm sorry, I don't have that much money. Would you settle for a used Kia?" No! Never!

You can never out-ask God. You ask Him for something and God says, "Is that all? I can do more!"

You don't ask Him to heal you and He unfortunately replies, "That is a big request. I can't heal you, but I can give you strength to bear the infirmity."

God is not like the joke I heard. God appeared to a man and told him, "Ask me for anything and I will give it to you."

The man thought about it and replied, "I want you to build a bridge across the ocean from California to Hawaii, so I can drive over anytime without flying."

God answered, "That is such a waste of man power and supply. Can't you think of something a little easier?"

So the man said, "Okay, how about making all the women in the world fall in love with me."

God stared at him and finally said, "Now, was that a two-lane or four-lane Bridge you wanted?"

No, that is small talk. God never answers your request by giving something smaller than what you asked. He is a big God and is rich. He owns the cattle on a thousand hills. His generosity is *immeasurably more than all we ask or imagine*. Although our faith can be measured, God's generosity cannot.

3. God gives to all.

The third truth mentioned in James is *God, who gives generously to all*. How many people does God give to? *To all*. God does not exclude anyone. He gives continually and generously to all. *For everyone who asks receives* (Luke 11:10). I know what you are thinking, *How can that be true, when so many people have never even been saved?*

Did you know that God provided salvation for the whole world? He paid the price for the sins of every sinner. Saint John says, *"He is the atoning sacrifice for our sins, and not only for ours but also for the sins of the whole world"* (I Jn 2:2). John wants you to know that God has given provision to save the whole world. Even though God knew that many would not accept His provision, He still gave His provision. The Calvinists who preach a limited atonement do not realize that God gives more grace than will be accepted.

He gives too much, which means a lot will be wasted. *Many times he delivered them, but they were bent on rebellion and they wasted away in their sin* (Ps 106:43).

God was delivering them, but *they wasted* their deliverance for their sin. What a waste! Many will waste God's generosity on their unbelief. God still gives to all, even the unbeliever. No one can say, "God did not give me anything." On the contrary, God has given you everything—salvation, health, prosperity, wisdom, strength, joy and peace. But are you wasting God's gifts?

4. God gives without finding fault.

James mentions one other factor in God's nature to give. *God, who gives generously to all without finding fault.* He is not looking for reasons not to give to you. He does not try to *find fault* with you. God is looking for every reason to give you His blessings.

He is not like a donor, who after being offended with the charity quits giving. He does not get easily offended. There is nothing you can do—good or bad—that will make God stop giving. He doesn't get mad and say, "That will be the last time I give him that gift!" No, He keeps on giving to all without finding fault with the recipient. You can't get God to stop giving.

Even as you read this book, He is giving you what you need. He is giving you strength, even though you don't deserve it. He is healing you, even though your bad health habits have brought your sickness. He is giving you wealth, even though you have squandered your money. He is giving you what you need, even though you don't deserve it. God is merciful. He does not give us what our deeds deserve.

Step Two:
GET RID OF YOUR DOUBTS

At this point you might be thinking, "This is too good to be true." When it seems too good to be true, then it is God! Based on these facts about the giving God, you would think there wouldn't be any lost, sick, or poor person on this earth, yet you know there are plenty of hurting and lost people. Why, if God is such a giver?

James explains why, *But when he asks, he must believe and not doubt, because he who doubts is like a wave of the sea, blown and tossed by the wind. That man should not think he will receive anything from the Lord* (James 1:6-7).

You *must believe and not doubt*. Doubt robs you of God's gifts. James even says concerning the doubter, *"That man should not think he will receive anything from the Lord."* Not only will he not receive wisdom, but he should not even think he would receive *anything* from the Lord. Notice the extreme positions: *"God gives, continually, and generously to all without finding fault"* yet he says to the doubter *"that man will not receive anything from God."* The doubter will not get a morsel from God. Not even a penny. Nothing. *Zippo. Nada.*

This was the situation with Israel. God had promised them the land of Canaan. However, the spies who were sent out did not believe it was possible to take the land.

But the men who had gone up with him said, "We can't attack those people; they are stronger than we are." And they spread among the Israelites a bad report about the land they had explored. They said, "The land we explored devours those living in it. All the people we saw there are of great size. We saw the Nephilim there (the descendants of Anak come from the Nephilim). We seemed like grasshoppers in our own eyes, and we looked the same to them" (Num 13:31-33).

Only two men thought it possible to take the land: Joshua and Caleb. *Joshua son of Nun and Caleb son of Jephunneh, who were among those who had explored the land, tore their clothes and said to the entire Israelite assembly, "The land we passed through and explored is exceedingly good. If the LORD is pleased with us, he will lead us into that land, a land flowing with milk and honey, and will give it to us. Only do not rebel against the LORD. And do not be afraid of the people of the land, because we will swallow them up. Their protection is gone, but the LORD is with us. Do not be afraid of them"* (Num 14:6-9).

Two out of twelve had faith. You don't find faith in too many people. Joshua and Caleb knew that God continually gives. They spoke as if God had already given them the land. *"Their protection is gone!"* The facts were the enemies had weapons and walls around their cities. Yet Joshua and Caleb knew that God had given before they could ask. Nevertheless, the majority ruled, and so Israel failed to take the promise land.

The Hebrew writer takes this story and applies it to the Christian: *So we see that they were not able to enter, because of their unbelief. Therefore, since the promise of entering his rest still stands, let us be careful that none of you be found to have fallen short of it. For we also have had the gospel preached to us, just as they did; but the message they heard was of no value to them, because those who heard did not combine it with faith* (Heb 3:19, 4:1-2).

This is not a story to be viewed without application. The same can happen to us, if we do not *combine the gospel preached to us with faith.* We have heard the gospel, but are we mixing it with our faith?

Israel was given the promise land. We have been given the land of promises. There are so many promises which God has given us, yet so few are enjoying them. Some even question God's promises. Some are not sure that all the promises belong to us. Some think certain promises belong to Israel or simply to the early church. This is not what the New Testament teaches. Until you are willing to accept the whole gospel as true, then you will never receive all the benefits of the gospel. Doubt will keep you from receiving all that God gives.

God requires Faith

Faith is the key to receiving from God, but if God requires that I have faith when it is unattainable for me to have it, then I have a right to challenge His fairness. But if He hands over to me the instrument whereby faith can be produced, then the responsibility rests with me whether or not I have faith. God has done just that. *So then faith cometh by hearing, and hearing by the word of God* (Romans 10:17, KJV). If I get the Word of God, then I get faith. If I get water, I get wet. Wet and water go hand in hand. So it is with faith. The key to faith is the Word of God. Let us look at what comprises the Word of God.

1. God has spoken to us through the prophets.

The Old Testament saints were without excuse when they heard the prophets. If they had not heard them, then they could not be blamed for not having faith.

2. God has spoken to us through His Son, Jesus Christ. Jesus is the Word of God made flesh.

Jesus words and example becomes for us the message from God.

3. God continues to speak to us through the Holy Spirit.

This is the most applicable for today, because we were not there with the prophets of old nor did we hear Christ teach or see Him act, so the only thing we have are the words of the prophets and the words and life of Christ in the Bible. The Bible is our link to their lives and messages.

Christ promised that the Holy Spirit *will guide you into all truth. He will not speak on his own; he will speak only what he hears, and he will tell you what is yet to come* (John 16:13).

The Holy Spirit inspired the apostles to write down the Word of God. For example, Paul's writings become Scripture as Peter mentions: *Paul's letters contain some things that are hard to understand, which ignorant and unstable people distort, as they do the other Scriptures, to their own destruction.*(2 Pet 3:16). Peter calls Paul's letters *other Scriptures*. The apostles' written words become the Word of God to us.

Paul affirms this in 1 Thessalonians 2:13: *And we also thank God continually because, when you received the word of God, which you heard from us, you accepted it not as the word of men, but as it actually is, the word of God, which is at work in you who believe.*

Skeptics attack the Bible more than any voice of God. They do not attack Christ or His message, but the instrument whereby His message comes to us—that is the Bible. Ironically, how is it that people claim to believe in Christ but deny the Bible which tells us about Him? The only authoritative and complete record of Christ is the Bible. To deny the Bible is to refute the only comprehensive story about Christ.

Tradition

The apostles both spoke and wrote. *So then, brothers, stand firm and hold to the teachings we passed on to you, whether by word of mouth or by letter* (2 Thess 2:15). Their words are the Word of God. However, the oral presentations are not preserved for us today. Only what they wrote is in our hands.

This bothers some people. They want to know what else, other than the Bible, did they teach. There is no point to speculate. We must go by what is written.

Jesus limited Himself to what was written. Consistently He said, "It is written." "Have you not read?" No doubt there were many other things that the prophets said, but we cannot know them unless they were written. The same is true of Christ and the apostles.

Some branches of Christianity believe that *traditions* are the oral teachings of the apostles. It is quite possible that some traditions that we have came directly from the apostles, but there are many others that clearly came *after* them. These would be man-made traditions.

Jesus warned about these kinds of traditions: *And he said to them: "You have a fine way of setting aside the commands of God in order to observe your own traditions!"* (MK 7:9). One way to determine whether a tradition possibly came directly from the apostles is if it affirms what is written. On the other hand, if it contradicts the written Word of God, then you can be assured that it did not come from the Apostles, and thus, is not the Word of God.

Catholic traditions such as prayers to the saints, novenas to the Virgin Mary, Pope as Vicar of Christ, salvation by works, and other such things are contradictory to the Bible and so they could not be the Word of God.

Protestant traditions such as the cessation of the gifts of the Spirit, once saved always saved, and belief that salvation is the same as the baptism in the Holy Spirit are also contradictory to the Scriptures and so would be categorize as man-made.

What is more reliable: the word written or the word spoken? Clearly when someone puts their words on paper, then we know for sure what they said. Contracts that are written are more reliable than oral contracts. If a written contract says that the agreed price was $100 but one party argued that they verbally agreed to a price of $200, unless the other party agrees, the written contract is the thing that will be enforced.

So it is with the Bible: it is *written* and so we know for sure what God says. No speculation as to what the apostles taught is admissible to our lives.

Someone who claims to have all the faith in the world, but does not know the Bible has deceived himself. The Bible is the thing that God placed in our hands to get faith. Ignoring it will be detrimental to your faith. Refusing to read it will obliterate your faith. Staying out of church where the Bible is preached and taught will keep you from getting faith.

Faith is a gift of God given to men only as they expose themselves, with all their hearts, to the truth of His Word. Simply reading it will not necessarily impart faith. Hearing sermons will not automatically produce faith. You must totally open yourself to the reality of God's Word. You must hear it as God speaking to you. You read it believing every word, although, you may not fully understand it or how to correctly apply it. In time, you will come to understand it.

Step Three:
BE CAREFUL WHO YOU LISTEN TO

As important as the Scriptures are, the actual determining factor to people's faith is what they hear in their pulpit at church. This is what Paul meant when he wrote, *Faith cometh by hearing the Word of God* (Rom 10:17). He was referring to the word that was *preached* not the Word that was *written*, for he writes, *How, then, can they call on the one they have not believed in? And how can they believe in the one of whom they have not heard? And how can they hear without someone preaching to them? And how can they preach unless they are sent? As it is written, "How beautiful are the feet of those who bring good news!"* (Rom 10:14-15).

Protestants, Catholics and non-denominational churches all use the Bible in their sermons, but you can see the difference between the churches — what they believe and practice. How is that possible? It's possible because what is preached in the churches is *more important* to the faith life of the congregants than what is in the scriptures. The Bible can say one thing, but if the minister says something else, then the members will believe more in what the clergy said than what God's Word says.

This is why an important step to receiving from God is to be part of a church that teaches and practices the Word of God and refuses to add man-made tradition that could affect negatively the faith of the people. Your faith may be built up by reading this book, but if you go back and continue to hear sermons that undermine your faith, then eventually, the Word you receive from this book will be uprooted.

Much of what is taught in the pulpit is not biblical. When preachers say tongues is of the devil, or healing passed away, or casting out demons were for a superstitious people, then you know the sermon is not the Word of God, and so people will not have faith to receive from God listening to those lies. Many sincere Christians sit in their churches under unbelief. The clergy doubt the Word or rationalize parts of it away. A church is the sum total of all that is preached behind their pulpits.

We must be like the Bereans who *were of more noble character than the Thessalonians, for they received the message with great eagerness and examined the Scriptures every day to see if what Paul said was true* (Acts 17:11). They did not blindly accept Paul's teachings. They were open-minded but not gullible. They *examined the Scriptures* not just a few times, but *every day to see if what Paul said was true.*

Often people think they don't have the time or education to examine the teachings of their church, but you are responsible to believe correctly the things of the gospel. You have no excuse. You can't argue, "But God, it's not my fault that I misbelieved the gospel. It's my churches fault for lying to me."

No! You have the Scriptures available to examine. If the Bereans, without the printing press and access to a lot of biblical material, could examine the teachings of Paul in light of the Scriptures, then so can you. Let me give you some examples how a church's teaching can undermine people's faith.

Do all Speak in Tongues?

One religious lady argued with me about speaking in tongues. She said, "You Pentecostals all speak in tongues, yet Paul asked, 'Do all speak in tongues?' It is clear from Paul's teachings that not everyone spoke in tongues, so you are wrong to expect everyone to speak in tongues."

I knew the denomination she was from and that they did not believe in tongues at all. So I asked her, "According to your argument, there should at least be some people who speak in tongues, so how many in your church speak in tongues?" After trying to side step my question, she admitted that no one spoke in tongues in her church.

Why didn't anyone speak in tongues in her house of worship? Because they were not taught that it was a gift from God. Even though speaking in tongues is available, and the scriptures encourage it, some will not experience it because they have not *heard* that it was for them.

The apostle Paul encountered some disciples and asked them, "Did you receive the Holy Spirit when you believed?"

They answered, "No, we have not even heard that there is a Holy Spirit." (Acts 19:2)

The gift was available to them all this time, but they failed to receive because they had not *heard* that there is a Holy Spirit. Today some have heard of the Holy Spirit, but they have not heard that they could receive Him in a personal way just like they received Christ, or that God would empower them as witnesses when they received.

Faith comes by hearing the Word, so Paul preached the Word to them, and when they were ready he *placed his hands on them, the Holy Spirit came on them, and they spoke in tongues and prophesied. There were about twelve men in all* (Acts 19:6-7). All twelve spoke in tongues, not one failed to receive the gift. Tongues are a sign gift for all.

Once a person receives tongues as a sign gift of the baptism in the Spirit, then they can use it in a private, devotional way in prayer. They may never be used to speak in tongues as a public message to the congregation. If they did, they or someone else would have to interpret so that others will be edified.

For example, most praying is done privately, but there are some prayers that are public. The same is true of speaking in tongues. Some tongues are messages from God. If anyone speaks in a tongue, two—or at the most three—should speak, one at a time, and someone must interpret. If there is no interpreter, *the speaker should keep quiet in the church and speak to himself and God* (1 Cor 14:28).

If you have a message in tongues that can be interpreted, then you may do it publicly, or else you should *keep quiet in the church*, you can still speak silently to yourself and to God.

I thank God that I speak in tongues more than all of you. But in the church I would rather speak five intelligible words to instruct others than ten thousand words in a tongue (1Cor 14:18). Paul spoke much in tongues, *more than all of* them, but he did not use it often in the church. This means tongues can be both a private, devotional verbal communication to God like prayer and a public message to the congregation.

Therefore tongues have a two fold purpose: a message to the people for public edification and speaking to God only for personal edification. *He who speaks in a tongue edifies himself* (1 Cor 14:4). Personal edification occurs when you do *not speak to men but to God* (1 Cor 14:2).

I've said all this to show the reason people have not received the baptism in the Holy Spirit with the confirmation of tongues. They have not received because they have not *heard* the Word of God which produces faith. *Does God give you his Spirit and work miracles among you because you observe the law, or because you believe what you heard?* (Gal 3:5). You get the Spirit by *believing what you heard*. Conversely, if you haven't heard, you cannot receive. The lady I mentioned did not receive tongues because of what she was taught. Of course, speaking in tongues is in the Bible, but faith comes usually when we hear it taught correctly from the pulpit.

Working of Miracles

Paul not only spoke of receiving the Spirit by faith, but also of God's willingness to *work miracles* because *you believe what you heard*. Many have not seen God's miracle power because, like tongues, they have not *heard* from the Word on this topic. They might have heard despairing remarks on the subject. They might have been told to stay away from "healers".

They have forgotten that "*In the church God has appointed first of all apostles, second prophets, third teachers, then workers of miracles, also those having gifts of healing*" (1 Cor 12:28). God has given some to work miracles and others with gifts of healing. It is biblical, but some doubt God's appointed ministers.

Where are these ministers to be found? *In the church God has appointed.* I find it amazing that some argue miracles and healings have passed away, yet they should have considered that God appointed in the church these ministry gifts of miracles and healings. God does not just perform miracles and healing, but He has given some the ability to bring the miracles and healing to others.

Conservative Christians will sometimes be open to the possibility that God could still heal and perform miracles, but they have difficulty believing God could *appoint workers of miracles* and *those with gifts of healing*. They balk at such a thought.

Many have come into my meetings and have witnessed people being healed and delivered from demons, yet they are very skeptical that God should choose to use me in this way. It is God's prerogative to put miracle workers and healers in the church. He did not ask your opinion if He should.

I have found that faith-filled people receive from God. Occasionally, I have seen skeptics healed, but generally the rule is people have to believe in order for them to receive healing and miracles from God. Here is a case in point:

Jesus went to His hometown, accompanied by His disciples.

When the Sabbath came, Jesus began to teach in the synagogue, and many who heard Him were amazed.

"Where did this man get these things?" they asked. "What's this wisdom that has been given Him, that He even does miracles! Isn't this the carpenter? Isn't this Mary's son and the brother of James, Joseph, Judas and Simon? Aren't His sisters here with us?" And they took offense at Him.

Jesus said to them, "Only in his hometown, among his relatives and in his own house is a prophet without honor." *He could not do any miracles there, except lay His hands on a few sick people and heal them. And He was amazed at their lack of faith* (Mark 6: 6).

Just like in our day, the people questioned a man's God-given ability to work miracles. They could not envision Jesus, with whom they grew up, being able to do miracles. They knew Jesus. He was a hometown boy! How could he do miracles? *And they took offense at him.* Because of the *lack of faith* Jesus *could not do any miracles there, except lay his hands on a few sick people and heal them* (Matt 13:57, 58).

If the people stopped the Son of God's power to do miracles, then isn't it possible for the same to happen today? Let us not question a person's anointing to heal, cast out demons and perform miracles, for if we do then doubt will cut us off from God's miracle supply.

People often question the anointing on ministers because they have not *heard* that God appointed in the church these officers. They know about teachers and administrators, but they have not heard about *workers of miracles* and *those with gifts of healing*.

Now that you know about these ministers, you can have faith God could use them to bless you. Until you know about them, you cannot have faith to receive them.

Cheese and crackers

One of my favorite illustrations which drives home this point is the story of Mr. Robinson. Robinson was a man who lived in a third world country. He heard about abundance in America, so he saved up everything he could to purchase a boat trip to America. As he boarded the ship, excitement filled his heart.

Since all he could afford was the ticket, he took along some cheese and crackers. At morning he took his cheese and unwrapped it, grabbed a dull knife and sliced a little for his stale crackers. He ate it. At noon he did the same. During dinner time he repeated the process.

Soon the trip became tiresome. He became so hungry. Finally, he could hold it back no longer; he left his cabin and took a peek in the dinning room, where the rich passengers enjoyed ham, sausage, eggs, biscuits and gravy. His mouth drooled. But after watching them eat, he went back to his cabin and began to eat the cheese and crackers.

At lunch he did the same; he peered through the windows of the dinning room and watched in envy the people consumed their meals. Succulent ham and perfectly carved roast with mash potatoes satisfied the people, but not for Robinson. He shrugged his shoulders and headed back to his cabin to eat the cheese and crackers.

Dinner was no different. This time he got closer and actually entered the dinning room. The odor of the food took him to heaven. Oh, it smelled so good. He watched the people break open the crabs and dip the sweet meat into the savory butter. Robinson wanted to eat the food so badly, but too bad for him, that he was so poor that he could only afford the ticket.

After the trip was over, Robinson quickly gathered his belongings to exit the ship, when the Captain noticed him, "Excuse me, sir. I make it a habit to know all my passengers by name through having a meal with them, yet I do not recall seeing you in the dinning room."

Robinson's eyes fell, he blushed, "Sir, I did not eat in the dinning room."

"Why, did someone offend you?"

"No, sir," Robinson continued, "You see, I only had enough money to buy the ticket, and I did not have enough to purchase any meals."

The Captain looked shocked, "But sir, did you not know that the meals were *included* in the price of the ticket?"

Many are like Mr. Robinson. They got the ticket of salvation Christ purchased for them. They know one day they will cross from this world into the next, but in this life they are often poor. They do not realize that the death of Christ provided not only a trip to heaven, but a wonderful banquet of blessings for us to enjoy.

God has set a table before us in the presence of our enemies (Psalm 23:5). But through listening to wrong teaching, many do not know that the baptism in the Spirit, divine healing, prosperity and deliverance has been included in the ticket of salvation. They are told everything will be theirs in the life to come, but for now, they must sacrifice.

Inheritance Now

The Hebrew writer makes it clear, *For this reason Christ is the mediator of a new covenant, that those who are called may receive the promised eternal inheritance — now that he has died as a ransom to set them free from the sins committed under the first covenant* (Heb 9:15). The *promised eternal inheritance* is not simply given in the age to come, but, rather, it is given *now that Christ has died.*

Can you imagine a rich uncle dying and you hear the will read, "I bequeath my entire estate to *your name,* and when you die, *you* get the inheritance."? Of course that sounds ludicrous. It is not your death that releases the inheritance; it is the death of the testator that puts the will into effect.

Yet Christianity has often preached a "pie in the sky" religion: *One day, when you die, you will receive all that God has for you.* Notice the emphasis is on the death of the testate and not the testator. Christianity is really about the death of Christ, not of the Christian. You don't get the inheritance *because* of your death, but of Christ' death!

The Hebrew writer continues: *In the case of a will, it is necessary to prove the death of the one who made it, because a will is in force only when somebody has died; it never takes effect while the one who made it is living* (9:16). A will is in force *when somebody who made it dies,* not the beneficiary's death. You are beneficiary of Christ' death and you receive the inheritance now, since Christ already died.

During the time when China cracked down hard on Christians, a woman took her two daughters to a house meeting. A soldier stopped them and asked the mother where she was going. She did not want to lie and yet she knew if she told him that they were going to Church then she would have been arrested and forced to reveal the location of the church.

She wisely responded, "My brother has died, and we are going to hear the reading of the will."

Praise God! She knew more about Christianity than most western Christians. This is the message of the Bible. This is why in the front of your Bible it says, **Old Testament** and when you move past it, it says **New Testament**. A testament is derived from the phrase, "Last Will and Testament." The Bible is the testament that Christ left. It reveals what He provided for us through His death.

Good preaching behind the pulpit will reveal your inheritance in Christ.

Bad preaching, however, will hinder you from receiving all God has for you. You cannot continue to stay in a church that compromises the gospel, and expect to receive everything God promised.

Jesus led the blind out

Jesus knew the importance of having a right, positive atmosphere in order to receive from God. There was a blind man from Bethsaida who was brought to Jesus so He could heal him. Jesus did not pray for the man at once, but instead *He took the blind man by the hand and led him outside the village. When he had spit on the man's eyes and put his hands on him, Jesus asked, "Do you see anything?"* (Mark 8:23). This is the only case where Jesus led the man out of his city. What was wrong with this town?

Jesus prophesied against it: "Woe to you, Korazin! Woe to you, Bethsaida! For if the miracles that were performed in you had been performed in Tyre and Sidon, they would have repented long ago, sitting in sackcloth and ashes" (Luke 10:13). The town of Bethsaida was saturated with unbelief. Jesus knew that in order to get this man to believe, He had to lead him out of this kind of negative, doubt-filled atmosphere.

This radical action was almost not enough, for the man did not receive his "complete" sight; he received only a partial healing. This is the only case in all of the gospels where a man received an unfinished cure.

I've heard critics of the healing revival say that Jesus healed everyone completely and instantly, but this case proves otherwise. *Once more Jesus put his hands on the man's eyes. Then his eyes were opened, his sight was restored, and he saw everything clearly. Jesus sent him home, saying, "Don't go into the village"* (Mark 8:25-26).

After laying hands a second time the man received his complete healing. It took Jesus twice to lay his hands on him to get him healed, because the man was influenced by his village. After he was healed, Jesus told him not to go back to his town. Jesus warned him that to return would be detrimental to his health. He could lose what he received if he went back to that wicked city.

The same is true of believers today. If you continue to attend a doubt-filled, skeptical church, then you will have difficulty receiving "complete" victory, or if you go back, you could lose what you have received.

I encourage you to attend a positive, uplifting church which believes all things are possible with God!

Step Four:
BELIEVE YOU RECEIVE

Faith is required to receive any benefit in this life. Hope is necessary to receive benefits in the life to come, yet when it comes to distinguishing the difference between faith and hope, few understand it.

Now faith is the substance of things hoped for, the evidence of things not seen (HEB 11:1, KJV). Often people interchange the word "faith" for "hope", but they are not the same. How could they be since faith is the substance of things hoped for? The New English Bible says: *Faith gives substance to the things we hope for.* You may hope for something — the baptism in the spirit, health, prosperity — but faith gives substance to it, which means, faith makes what you hope for come true. You may hope against hope, but until you *believe* then you will not receive.

Remember Abraham, *Against all hope, Abraham in hope believed and so became the father of many nations* (Rom 4:18). Abraham did not see the promise of God fulfilled simply because he *hoped against all hope.* The Bible says that *Abraham in hope believed.* He did not simply *hope*, he *believed.* Belief is the verb form of the noun faith. He had to have faith as well as hope.

You can hope and hope, but until you have faith, your hopes will not come to pass.

Here is another clear passage which shows that faith and hope are not the same. *And now these three remain: faith, hope and love. But the greatest of these is love* (1Cor 13:13). He numbered these virtues, *three*. Not two, but three. By calling them three that would mean faith and hope could not be the same virtue.

One distinct difference is that faith and hope operate in different time zones. Hope is in the future, faith is in the present. *For in this hope we were saved. But hope that is seen is no hope at all. Who hopes for what he already has? But if we hope for what we do not yet have, we wait for it patiently* (Rom 8:24-25). Hope does not have anything now, but waits in the future for it.

Contrast that with faith: *Now faith is the assurance (the confirmation, the title deed) of the things [we] hope for* (Heb 11:1, Amp). You get a *title deed* for the thing you currently own. For example, you purchase a car from a dealer and place a down payment. You are not given the title until it is completely paid for. You may claim it is your car, but it really is not yours until it is paid off, and then the bank sends you a title deed. At that time you own it. The title deed is proof it is yours.

Faith can only trust God for the things that can be obtained in this life. Faith is the ingredient to receive the things promised in this age—salvation, the Holy Spirit, good health, peace and many other present blessings.

Hope waits for the things God has promised will come later, such as the rapture. Paul writes:

while we wait for the blessed hope — the glorious appearing of our great God and Savior, Jesus Christ (Tit 2:13). Jesus will come back at the end of this age, so we cannot "exercise our faith" to bring Him back. Whether we believe He is coming is irrelevant. He is coming back! His return is called the *blessed hope*. Not the blessed faith, but hope. Hope looks for the future glory that will be revealed; faith claims the present glory that is available in this life.

Jesus Teaching on Faith

Look carefully at our wonderful Lord's teaching on the present tense of faith: *"Have faith in God," Jesus answered. "Therefore I tell you, whatever you ask for in prayer, believe that you have received it, and it will be yours"* (Mk 11:22, 24).

The impact of this promise should grip any sincere believer. The riches in this passage are absolutely enormous. The simplicity and subtlety are both transparent.

The promise is simple: you simply need to ask and believe.

The subtlety is tricky: you mustn't simply believe that God will give you the answer, but you must believe He has *already* given you the answer — before you can see any evidence of it.

It is the subtlety of this passage that many glance over. They hope and pray! Unfortunately they confuse faith with hope. They think because they have some expectation that God will someday give them the answer that they really believe. They are not believing, but hoping. Jesus said, "Have faith in God." He is not talking about hope, but faith.

Faith believes *you have received it, and it will be yours.*

Four facts

There are four obvious facts about the present tense of faith:

1. Faith believes before it receives.

Many want to believe when they see, but faith works in reverse. You must believe if you want to see.

There is a story in the Old Testament that shows this truth. Israel had experienced severe famine. The bread lines were long, and the bread was scarce — and expensive. The word of the Lord came to Elisha and gave him a promise that bread would be real cheap. An officer of the king said, "Look, even if the LORD should open the flood-gates of the heavens, could this happen?"

The man of God had replied, "You will see it with your own eyes, but you will not eat any of it!" *And that is exactly what happened to him, for the people trampled him in the gateway, and he died* (2 Ki 7:20). The officer did not get to enjoy the blessings of God because he did not believe. Many have this kind of faith: *I'll believe it when I see it.* That may work fine in the world, but it does not work well with God. God wants us to believe before we see.

Thomas once had this kind of attitude: "*Unless I see the nail marks in his hands and put my finger where the nails were, and put my hand into his side, I will not believe it.*" (Jn 20:25) We don't call him "Doubting Thomas" for nothing. Yet, many doubt like he did. They want to *feel* and *see* before they believe.

Later Jesus appeared before Thomas. He grabbed his hand and forced him to touch his side, "Stop doubting and believe." I could see Thomas trying to pull his hand away, but the Lord made him confront his doubts. Finally he exclaimed, "My Lord and my God!"

Don't be forced to believe by having to see. Be willing to believe before you see.

For example, many Christians doubt their salvation because they do not "feel" the same as they once did. Unfortunately they are going by their feelings, not their faith. As long as their feelings become supreme, they are likely to backslide and worse, go too far and become an apostate.

The same mistake is made when it comes to the baptism in the Holy Spirit; people want God to make them feel something before they believe in it. Some have said, "Well, if speaking in tongues is of God, then God knows where I live, and He can give it to me anytime He wants. I'm open."

The truth is they are not open. For them to receive they must believe in speaking in tongues before they can speak. Some try to test God, "Okay, Lord, I really am not sure about all this, but I will pray and ask you to give it to me if it is real." Then when nothing happens, they assume tongues is not real or not for them.

They are waiting for some sign or feeling that it is real. However, it *is* legitimate because Jesus promised the Spirit. The Spirit has come and will fill anyone who wants all of the Spirit. You must believe first, then you will receive.

2. Faith receives at the instant it believes.

F. B Meyer translates Mark 11:24: *"What things so ever you desire, when you pray, believe that you have taken it."* When is the answer yours, before or after you have seen the answer? You must believe it is yours at the moment you have believed. Believing makes you a receiver.

Joshua was given the reign of leadership after Moses' death. He had his first test as the newly appointed head. How was he going to conquer the biggest city in the promise land?

As he contemplated this massive undertaking an angel of the Lord appeared to him and told him, *"See, I have delivered Jericho into your hands, along with its king and its fighting men"* (Jos 6:2). Jericho was still standing when the angel made this statement. The angel was speaking in the present tense even though the walls were still surrounding Jericho.

Joshua had to believe that Jericho was theirs before he could see it falling. The same must be true of successful pastors. They must believe their church is growing even if they do not see their numbers growing. Just because nothing is happening now does not mean God is not working.

I have learned to believe for success regardless of what I am currently seeing. What I see is subject to change, but God's Word will never change. He has declared that the Church of Jesus Christ is like a mustard seed and it grows to become the largest garden plant. True leaders take up Joshua's view point: they believe the city they reside in is theirs even if few show up to church.

My declaration of faith is, "*Almost the whole city is gathering to hear the word of the Lord*" (Acts 13:44).

I believe it. It is God's Word. I may not see it right now, but I will see it, because I believe. It seems quite impossible to believe that a city can be won to the Lord, but it can. It was impossible for walls to tumble down solely by the power of God, but it happened to Jericho.

It occurred when the people gave a loud shout. They shouted, "*For the LORD has given you the city!*" (Jos 6:16) As they shouted, the walls fell. They did not wait for the walls to fall, and then shout victory. Victory must be received at the instant you believe.

Another story vividly illustrates this second principle. Jesus was in a synagogue teaching the word, when a woman caught His eye. Her back was deformed. She was known in the whole city as a "cripple" but not to Jesus. He saw something else. He did not see a cripple but a daughter of Abraham.

"*Woman, you are set free from your infirmity,*" Jesus boldly declared (Luke 13:12). Notice carefully His exact words: He saw her free before anyone else did. She did not look free! Jesus did not promise her freedom in some indefinite future time, but said that she was free now! Afterward *he put his hands on her, and immediately she straightened up and praised God* (v. 13).

Many lay hands on the sick hoping that God will heal them in his perfect timing, but few understand the Jesus-Principle of laying hands on the sick. He saw everyone healed before it was manifested.

I had done a study on the ministry of healing from the life of Christ, and I noticed that Jesus never asked anyone to declare their infirmities or their problems. He did not ask a sick person, "So, what's wrong with you?" Yet, that is the common question that ministers ask before prayer.

Instead Jesus asked, "What do you want me to do for you?" That is a far different question than asking them, "What is wrong with you?" Jesus wanted them to believe *not* in what they could see, but what God had said was reality. He did not *see* cripples or blind people. He saw them whole. To a man who was paralyzed He told him, "Pick up your mat and go home." He believed in the man's health, even if it looked like he was sick.

To a woman who looked like a prostitute, he said, "Your sins are forgiven." She had not changed her seductive clothes to more modest ones. She looked the same to everyone, but not to Christ. He declared her forgiven, even if one could not see the immediate change.

He smiled, *"Your faith has saved you; go in peace"* (Lk 7:50). Did others applaud? No, they did just the opposite. Some questioned Jesus discernment; others thought He had blasphemed God to make such a bold pronouncement.

Today people do the same. A very wicked person can come forward in church and pray for forgiveness. And what should the minister say? The same that Christ said, "Your sins are forgiven." Others criticize the minister for promising salvation without proof. What evidence do we have that they are forgiven? They have not yet proven their repentance with good deeds, but we accept their forgiveness at the instant of the sinner's faith. We do not need evidence. We take it by faith. Faith receives at the instant it believes.

3. Faith must act as though the answer is given.

Suppose you prayed for $500 and while you were praying someone handed you the money, what would your response be? That is how you should act the moment you have believed God.

If you believe that you have taken the answer when you pray, then you will stop worrying over the situation. You will be joyful and happy. There will be a note of praise in your speech. However, if you are still fearful, unhappy, and critical of your circumstances, then you are not acting as though the answer is given.

Pastor if you believe your church is growing, then you will build!

Bible school student, if you believe God has filled you with the Spirit, then you will witness.

Wife, if you believe that God has changed your husband, then you will treat him with respect and kindness.

Child of God if you believe God has forgiven you, then you will serve worthily in your church.

If you believe God has set you free from the fear of flying, then you will board the airplane.

There is no point to pretend that we believe when we refuse to act as though the answer is given.

Ask and keep on asking?

Consider also how you should pray if you believed you had received the answer. Should you continue petitioning God for the same thing or should you change the way you pray? Some people think you should continue asking God over and over again. However, Jesus warned against this type of attitude: *"Don't recite the same prayer over and over as the heathen do, who think prayers are answered only by repeating them again and again"* (Matt 6:7-8, Living).

Others have ignored this warning based on a faulty understanding of certain statements and parables that Christ gave. Example: *"Ask and it will be given you"* (Luke 11:9). The Amplified Bible reads, "Ask *and* keep on asking." The assumption is to keep asking for the same thing over and over again. On top of these statements Jesus gave a couple of parables to illustrate the need to persevere:

He told about the unjust judge who finally gave in to the widow because she pestered him to death. And then He told about a man coming to his friend at midnight asking for bread, and because he kept disturbing him the friend finally got out of bed and gave him what he wanted.

Because of these two parables, some have assumed that we should keep asking God for the same thing over and over again. These statements and parables are not meant to teach that we should ask for the same thing over and over again, but rather that we should always keep praying.

Then Jesus told his disciples a parable to show them that they should always pray and not give up (LK 18:1).

"Prayer" is the subject, not "petitioning". People assume that prayer is only "petition". There is so much more to prayer than that. The Apostle Paul mentioned: *And pray in the Spirit on all occasions with all kinds of prayers and requests* (Ep 6:18). There are different kinds of prayers. Some are petitions, others intercessions, still others thanksgiving. Jesus is teaching about the need to keep on praying, not to keep on "petitioning" God for the same thing.

The Bible tells us how to petition God: *Do not be anxious about anything, but in everything, by prayer and petition, with thanksgiving, present your requests to God* (Phil 4:6).

There are different ways to pray other than asking. According to this passage we should present our request *with* thanksgiving. We thank God for what He has given us. In other words, while we pray and ask God for something we should believe that we receive it, so it is natural to thank God for it in advance.

Suppose someone promised me a dinner at the end of the week. Would I say to him, "Well, when I eat the meal I will thank you for it."?

No! I would immediately thank him for the meal, even though I had not eaten any of it. What if at the end of the first day I call him on the phone and say, "Now, brother, you remember the meal you promised? Are you still taking me out to eat?" He would consider that a strange call. Later, at four in the morning I wake him up, "Brother, I woke up early thinking about the meal you promised. Is it still on?" For sure, he would think I was crazy.

Unfortunately, that is how many approach petitions. They keep asking God for the same thing over and over again. However, instead of asking God again and again, and sounding doubtful, why not thank God for the answer? Rejoice in the Lord! Tell the Lord how grateful you are that He has answered your prayer. Take the full armor of God and cut the devil inside and out. Release your angels to work for you. Stand on God's Word! This brings us to the fourth and final principle of the present tense of faith.

4. Faith meets the battle of the time lapse.

There is almost always a period between the time you believe you receive the answer and the time it manifests. This period is called the battle of the time lapse.

The Literal Greek says, *"What things soever you desire, when you pray, go on believing that you have received them, and you shall have them"* (Mark 11:24). Since most of the things we are trusting God for often take some time for them to manifest, we can easily get discouraged and stop believing. Yet, Jesus said to *go on believing.*

You cannot expect to receive from God if you begin in faith but end in unbelief. The story of Peter walking on water is a good illustration that proves this point. Peter started in faith by walking on the water, but later, his faith was replaced with fear and he began to sink. You see, you cannot receive from God if you give up your faith. You must begin in faith and end in it. Only if you end in it will you receive what God promised.

Consider the length of time it took God to create the worlds. It took six days, so this tells us that God does not do things instantly. Someone might complain, "Yea, but my problem is not that hard for God to fix, why does He take so long? It has been longer than six days." Remember that God does not count like we do.

It reminds me of a guy who prayed, "Lord, is it true that a million years is like a second to you?"

God replied, "Yes, my son."

"And is it true that a million dollars is like a penny to you."

"Yes, my son."

The man then asked, "Could I have a penny?"

The Lord responded, "Sure, in *a second*."

It is hard to laugh when the answer seems to take long. How we respond during the battle of the time lapse will determine whether or not we will ultimately receive from God. This period is so important that we will deal with it in length in the next chapter.

Step Five:
BE PREPARED FOR A BATTLE

Society is in a hurry. They want things quickly. They hate to wait. Businesses understand our impatience so they capitalize on it. They provide one hour photo; glasses in an hour. Grocery stores have express lanes. Restaurants promise fast food or it's free.

My wife and I were eating at a restaurant that promised the food in ten minutes or it's free. Sure enough, they were late by a couple of minutes. We enjoyed the food for free. I must admit I felt bad for the waitress so I gave her a large tip.

I bring this up because this impatience has translated over to our relationship with God. If we do not receive from God right away, then we are quick to abandon our faith and go back into the world. At the very least, if we do not receive from God according to our time table, then we silently become discouraged and lose our zeal for God.

The scriptures are quite clear on this point: *We do not want you to become lazy, but to imitate those who through faith and patience inherit what has been promised* (Heb 6:12). It is not just faith that is necessary to receive from God, but patience as well. Simply because you have not seen the answer yet, does not mean it will not come. You must be patient, which means, you must persevere and keep on believing you have the answer, despite the fact you cannot see it.

Laissez-faire

The subject of patience has been misunderstood by the body of Christ. Most view patience as an inactive trait. We see someone who is in a slow grocery store line and says nothing. We believe that to be patience. Or someone who is in heavy traffic and does not honk his horn. So we think that is patience. We have unwittingly associated patience with inactivity. To do nothing is patience, we think.

Actually, biblical patience is the opposite. Patience is "activity" toward the desired end. Notice again what the Hebrew writer says, *"We do not want you to become lazy"* then he mentions the need for patience. Patience must not be associated with laziness.

During the mid-nineteen century, when America's economy was in bad shape, the politicians had adopted a *laissez-faire* approach. It is French for "let things alone; let it be." Those who held to this philosophy believed that the market—buying and selling; free and fair competition—would fix itself of any economic problems. No government intervention was necessary. Eventually, they saw that they were wrong. Without the government's involvement—rules against monopolies, favors to private enterprises, corporate privileges—the economy would never bounce back and perhaps be irrevocably damaged.

I brought this up because many have the same poor understanding of patience. They think it means to let things alone; let things be. If God wants to let me stay sick, then I will patiently let it be. Wrong! True patience is best understood by the word "perseverance." *So do not throw away your confidence; it will be richly rewarded. You need to persevere so that when you have done the will of God, you will receive what he has promised* (Heb 10:35-36).

True perseverance "works" at "doing the will of God" rather than letting things alone, letting things be.

Jesus gave two parables about perseverance: A widow woman who kept badgering the judge until he gave her what she wanted, and a man who constantly banged on the door of a friend asking for bread. In both cases, neither person had a *laissez-faire* attitude; they had the opposite. They refused to accept disappointment. They kept at it until they got what they wanted. This is true biblical patience.

Who is Slow?

People have trouble doing this because of a lack of understanding how God works. They assume God is taking His "sweet" time, when in reality, He is not the one who is slow. He already arrived with the answer. He is now waiting on us to get ourselves in the right position to receive it. Let me prove this.

But do not forget this one thing, dear friends: With the Lord a day is like a thousand years, and a thousand years are like a day. The Lord is not slow in keeping his promise, as some understand slowness. He is patient with you, not wanting anyone to perish, but everyone to come to repentance (2 Pet 3:8-9).

Who is the patient one? God *is patient with you.* It only seems from our perspective that we are the ones that must be patient. However, we have to wait not because God has not yet answered, but because we have not yet been in the right position to receive. There are legitimate reasons why it *appears* that God is slow.

1. God tells time differently than we do.

As Einstein demonstrated, time is relative. His theory of relativity states that time must have a frame of reference, and that time is relative based on one's reference point.

Do you remember watching the film in school of a family being shot in a rocket at the speed of light? Time stopped for the family but time continued for those on earth. A hundred years went by and they returned to the earth still at their age, while everyone they knew had died of old age. For the family in the rocket it felt like a second in space, but for those on earth it felt like a hundred years.

Now consider God! God is light. His reference point of time is different from ours. He says, "*Now is the time of salvation*" (2 Cor 6:1) but many do not get saved until later. Who is really the one who is slow? Isn't it us who *waited* to get saved, instead of being saved *now*!

God does not delay. We are the ones who delay the answers.

2. God must work with our wills to bring about the fulfillment of His promises.

When you stand on God's promises, often God must work with others in order to answer your prayers. For example, if you are trusting God to prosper your church, then God must speak to the members to give generously. God cannot just wire money to your account. He must get it to you through people.

There are pastors who refuse to teach their members on tithing, either because they think it is not New Testament or they don't want to be viewed as greedy. However, God's appointed method of providing for the church is the members. God does not rain money out of the sky. If He did, He would be a counterfeiter.

God cannot violate free will, so He cannot make anyone give. He *can* inspire them, influence them, and yet leave it with them whether or not they want to give. So instead of thinking that God is slow, I think it is better stated that we are slow.

There are many examples we could give that could illustrate this truth, but there are also areas, such as healing or the baptism in the Spirit that do not seem to require other people to bring the answer. The truth is, even those areas, to a certain degree, require others.

For example, God may use a minister to bring the gift of healing to the sick, however, if the minister is not walking in faith and obedience this could hinder the sick from being healed. Consider how the disciples failed to heal the young boy because they lacked faith. Jesus took over the situation and eventually brought healing to the boy.

What would have happened if Jesus had not been there? Perhaps the boy would not have recovered, and others could have assumed that God had failed, when in reality it was the disciples that had failed.

3. God must answer according to the strength of one's faith.

We have already proven that God works through our faith. Some people's faith is weak, others strong. The strength of one's faith will determine how long the answer will take.

People have criticized the ministry of deliverance because we in that ministry often take longer to help people get healed. The critics often point out how quickly Jesus healed people. I agree that He did, but His faith was stronger than ours.

The Bible mentions "little faith" and "weak faith". Not all faith is equal. The level of faith determines the promptness of the answers from God.

4. God must work with our prayers to defeat the forces of darkness.

The devil will try to hinder God's promises from being fulfilled. He did this with Daniel. Daniel was the leading Jew among Israel and he needed to know some answers from God for his people, so he began to pray and fast.

Twenty one days later the angel appeared to him and said, *"Do not be afraid, Daniel. Since the first day that you set your mind to gain understanding and to humble yourself before your God, your words were heard, and I have come in response to them. But the prince of the Persian kingdom resisted me twenty-one days. Then Michael, one of the chief princes, came to help me, because I was detained there with the king of Persia"* (Dan 10:12-13).

Please notice that Daniel's prayer was heard instantly, but the forces of darkness prevented the answer from coming right away. If Daniel had stopped praying, then the angel would not have had the ammunition to defeat the spiritual *prince of the Persian kingdom.*

The Bible is clear; we must put on the full armor of God to take our stand of faith. The devil will throw everything at us to discourage us, but we must not give up.

5. God works on our character during times of apparent delays.

God is more interested in what you are **becoming** than what you are **receiving**. Apparent delays often teach us very important lessons: one of them is perseverance. James 1:2-4 says, *"Consider it pure joy, my brothers, whenever you face trials of many kinds, because you know that the testing of your faith develops perseverance. Perseverance must finish its work so that you may be mature and complete, not lacking anything."*

Observe the results of patience: you will *be mature and complete, not lacking anything.* Not only will the answer eventually come, but in the process of waiting for it, you personally become spiritually mature. God is interested more than simply you receiving what you desire; He wants you to grow. One way for you to grow is through testing.

Here is how it works: during times when it seems like the answer will not come, we usually begin to search our souls. Isn't that right? We know there must be something in us that has hindered the answer. So after discovering areas in us that are not right with God we begin the process of repentance, even over seemingly little things. However, if the answer had come quickly, we likely would have become spoiled. So God allows times of testing to make us tough.

Paul said it this way: *We also rejoice in our sufferings, because we know that suffering produces perseverance; perseverance, character; and character, hope* (Rom 5:3-4).

How can Paul and James both tell us to rejoice in sufferings and trials? Because there is an accomplishment that these difficulties achieve: they first produce perseverance and second perseverance produces character.

On the other hand, if you do not improve in character you will continue to struggle. You will fail to receive the blessing you have sought. It is better to make the changes now, so you can receive the blessing quicker.

In school when you take the final exam, if you do not pass you have to take the test again. The same is true with God. Until you pass the spiritual test, you will not be promoted.

I heard the story of a little Indian, who found a chick's egg that was ready to hatch. As he watched the little chick try to break open the shell and find her freedom, the little Indian felt bad for her struggle, so he cracked open the shell for the little bird. It was freed only to find that it was too weak to survive.

You see, the little boy did not realize that through struggle the chick was gaining strength to live. By short-circuiting the pathway of struggle, the chick did not have strength to survive. The same is true with our relationship with God. God could give everything to us right away, but we would not develop the strength of character to really enjoy the gifts He provides. So through perseverance, we develop the character we need to wisely use the gifts God gives.

You say to me, "But Pastor Tom, I have repented of everything I know that I have done, and yet the answer still has not come. What then?"

Good Fight of Faith

1 Timothy 6:12 says to fight the good fight of faith. If living by faith was easy and the results instant, then there would be no need to fight the good fight of faith. Doubt, fear and unbelief are great adversaries to faith. They usually get stronger when the answer takes longer.

How do you fight the good fight of faith during long delays in God's fulfillment of His promises? It's easy to live by faith when God answers quickly. But what happens when the answer takes a long time in coming? Do you give up? Of course not! But what do you do in the meantime?

The answer is here in 1Timothy 6:12: *Fight the good fight of the faith. Take hold of the eternal life to which you were called when you made your good confession in the presence of many witnesses.*

And Paul reminds us of Christ' example in fighting the good fight of faith: *Christ Jesus, who while testifying before Pontius Pilate made the good confession* (v. 13).

Finally Paul exhorts us to *keep this command without spot or blame until the appearing of our Lord Jesus Christ* (v. 14). What command are we to keep? The command to fight the good fight of faith is to be kept. And how do we fight the good fight of faith? Simple, we fight the good fight of faith by maintaining our good confession of faith.

You see the adversaries to your faith want to control your tongue. The adversaries want you speak doubt, fear and unbelief. They want you to make a bad confession.

A bad confession is based on the troubles and problems that you have gone through. Isn't that what you are tempted to do when you are surrounded by trouble? You want to complain! You want to blame! You want to scream! But you know that God has promised to come through and get you out of the pit you're in! Just hold on! Keep confessing God's Word! It will come to pass if you don't give up!

You say, "If I kept confessing that I'm healed and prosperous even though the facts say different, then wouldn't I be lying?" I would answer, How can you lie by saying the truth? God's Word is truth. In fact, it is the highest form of reality.

Face the Facts

The answer to this dilemma is found in the story of Abraham. At the age of seventy-five, God promised him a son, but it took twenty-five years before the promise came to pass. What did Abraham do during this interim period?

Romans 4:18-20 tells us: *"Against all hope, Abraham in hope believed and so became the father of many nations, just as it had been said to him, 'So shall your offspring be.' Without weakening in his faith, he faced the fact that his body was as good as dead...Yet he did not waver through unbelief regarding the promise of God."*

I want you to notice that Abraham did not pretend that he was physically able to procreate. The Bible says that he *faced the fact* that he was impotent. He did not pretend to be a young, sex-crazed bachelor. No! He faced the fact that he was so old that he wasn't interested in sex anymore. And even if he was interested in it, his wife surely wouldn't cooperate, or if she did, she definitely wouldn't get pregnant.

So how was Abraham going to walk by faith? First, he *faced the facts*. Before you know where you want to go, you must find out where you are. This is the starting point of faith. This is facing the facts. But you don't stop here. If you do, then you are in unbelief.

What are facts anyway? I like to use the word "f-a-c-t" as an acronym for False Appearance Contradicting Truth.

Many people confuse fact with truth. They are not the same. Facts can change; truth does not.

Facts relate to situations and circumstances; truth relates to God's Word. Jesus prayed and said, "Thy Word is truth!" God's Word is truth, but a doctor's report reveals only facts. A bank statement tells you the facts only, not the truth.

A doctor's diagnosis can change depending on how the patient responds. If his diagnosis can change, then it is not truth but fact. Yet God's Word continues to say, *By Jesus' stripes, I am healed* (1 Peter 2:24). It will read that way no matter how I feel. It will read that way today, tomorrow and to the next generation after us. It will always say I am healed. It is truth! Truth never changes.

A bank statement may show a negative cash flow one month and then show a positive cash flow the next month. In other words, a bank statement fluctuates depending on the customer's income and outgo. The statement shows only the facts. Yet God's Word continues to say, *My God shall supply all my needs according to His riches in glory by Christ Jesus* (Philippians 4:19). It will say that today as well as tomorrow. I can count on this scripture never changing. Men's opinion may change, but God's Word endures forever.

This is what Paul meant in Romans 3:4, *Let God be true, and every man a liar.* God's promises are permanent and reliable.

Can you see the difference between fact and truth?

A Good Confession is not Lying

Let me show you how Christ maintained His good confession, even though the facts said differently.

Jesus was being tried in court by Pontius Pilate. Attempting to get Jesus to respond, Pilate said, "You are a king, then!"

Jesus answered, "You are right in saying I am a king. In fact, for this reason I was born, and for this I came into the world, to testify to the truth. Everyone on the side of truth listens to Me."

Christ spoke the truth by declaring Himself to be king. Yet, factually His enemies could have argued with Him saying, "If you are king, why are you being tried? If you are king, where is your throne? If you are really king, why don't you rule?"

The point I'm bringing is this: Christ did not look like a king, but in the heavenly places He was king. And in time, His kingdom would be manifested to the world. After two thousand years, over two billion people on this earth today claim that Jesus is their king, and more people every day are coming to realize this.

But how many people today claim that Pilate or Caesar is their king? None. You see, the fact was clear, Caesar was king, but the truth was Jesus was king. Truth won. Facts lost.

Jesus made the good confession as to who He was, even though it did not look factual. But facts changed. Now more people claim to follow Christ than anyone who has ever lived. Christ' confession changed the world.

He is our pattern. We, too, can make our confession as to who we really are—new creatures, righteous, saints, healed, prosperous, wise, victorious, world over comers—and by doing this, we can change our own individual worlds.

We don't deny the facts, we simply believe the facts will change—and truth will prevail. And because we know the power of God's Word, we can face the facts and say, "Yes, the facts are that I'm feeling sick and my bills are piling up, yet the truth is, I'm healed and blessed."

When we know God's Word will prevail, we can go to the doctor and ask him for the facts. We can talk with our creditors and tell them the facts. But in all this, we know deep within our hearts the truth. It is only a matter of time before the truth wins and the facts lose.

My concern is for Christian people who are terrified of the facts. Consequently, they refuse to go to the doctor, claiming that they are healed, when in reality they are scared of finding out the facts—perhaps they have cancer or some incurable disease. Or they refuse to adjust their financial lifestyle claiming God will supply their need, but really they want God to supply their greed.

You see, when it dawns on you that facts will change, yet God's Word will not, then you can face the facts with God's Word knowing that His Word will prevail!

Step Six:
OVERCOME THE FEAR OF THE VISIBLE

You have confessed health, yet the doctors have told you the cancer has grown. You have confessed increase but the church has lost members. You have confessed prosperity, but the creditors are constantly harassing you.

What are you feeling? Probably fear. The real enemy to the battle of the time lapse is fear.

Fear is the opposite of faith. You might have thought doubt was its counterpart. It is in a technical sense. Doubt is an antonym for faith; however, most people think doubt only means to be uncertain about the truth.

There are two kinds of doubts: first is when you do not accept God's evidence presented or the testimony of a gospel witness; second when you fear evidence or testimony that is contrary to the Word of God.

Let us look at the first form of doubt. Thomas did not accept the testimony of the resurrection. Afterward, when Jesus appeared to him, He told him, *"Stop doubting and believe"* (John 20:27).

Later Jesus appeared to the Eleven as they were eating; he rebuked them for their lack of faith and their stubborn refusal to believe those who had seen him after he had risen (Mark 16:14). So here are two examples of doubt based on rejection of divine evidence or heavenly testimony.

The other kind of doubt is related to fear of physical evidence. If you look at the definition of doubt in a dictionary, another meaning would be "to fear or to be apprehensive about something."

If you were to ask sincere believers if they ever doubt, many would say no. If on the other hand, you ask them if they ever become fearful or apprehensive about something, nearly everyone would say yes. Let us talk about this kind of doubt.

Peter Sinks

Jesus had walked on the water when Peter cried out, "Lord, if it's you tell me to come to you on the water." Jesus told him to come.

Then Peter got down out of the boat, walked on the water and came toward Jesus. But when he saw the wind, he was afraid and, beginning to sink, cried out, "Lord, save me!" Immediately Jesus reached out his hand and caught him. "You of little faith," he said, "why did you doubt?" (Matt 14:29-31)

Jesus did not simply accuse Peter of doubt, but he asked a question about it: "Why did you doubt?" He wanted Peter to know the cause of his doubt. What caused him to doubt? Did an agnostic talk with him and put seeds of doubt in his mind? Did he doubt that Jesus had told him to come on the water? No, so why did he doubt?

He doubted because *he saw the wind,* and *he was afraid.* The thing that made Peter doubt was something visible. He saw the wind and felt the waves and so he was afraid. Jesus called his fear — doubt!

The most often repeated commandment in the Bible is "Fear not!" God does not tell the believer, "Doubt not." Doubt in terms of skepticism is not his problem. Doubt is the problem of the unbeliever. Fear however, is something every sincere believer has experienced.

What believer can honestly say he has never feared since becoming saved? He remembers the bad news he heard, and he recalls that fear was his first response. We all have felt it. I have!

Yet, deep within our hearts, we know fear is wrong. We can even say it is a sin! Fear is so sinful that God even says, *"The fearful, and unbelieving, and the abominable, and murderers, and whoremongers, and sorcerers, and idolaters, and all liars, shall have their part in the lake which burneth with fire and brimstone: which is the second death"* (Rev 21:8, KJV).

I understand the *unbelieving* go to hell, but why the *fearful*? Because fear is the opposite of faith. Both the *unbelieving* and *fearful* deserve hell. This word fearful can also be understood to mean cowardly. In fact, some translations use that word instead. You can understand this better.

A coward's greatest fear is death. He fears the worse may happen. Whenever he fears the worse, then he is a coward. Also the courageous child of God believes the best will happen. As long as he is optimistic he does not fear. Oh, he may feel the pressure of the situation, but he does not fear! He refuses to give into his fear and speak failure. He refuses to plan for the worse, because he knows God is on his side.

So what is the origin of this kind of fear? It is based on the "visible." A person fears only what he *sees*. If the doctor had told him the cancer was shrinking, then he would have rejoiced. If new members were added to the church, then the pastor would have been excited. If the poor man had come into a large sum of money, then he would have celebrated.

But no, they "saw" something to make them afraid. This is what makes this kind of fear so terrible to God. God is "unseen" and so when we become afraid of what we "see" we are making the "seen" to be more real than the "unseen." We believe more in the seen than in God!

Saw the Giants

Here is a great biblical story that illustrates the awfulness of fearing the visible. *But the men who had gone up with him said, "We can't attack those people; they are stronger than we are." And they spread among the Israelites a bad report about the land they had explored. They said, "The land we explored devours those living in it. All the people we saw there are of great size. We saw the Nephilim there (the descendants of Anak come from the Nephilim). We seemed like grasshoppers in our own eyes, and we looked the same to them"* (Num 13:31-33).

Notice the problem with the doubting spies — they *saw* the people *of great size*. They did not argue whether or not the land was truly plenteous as God had promised. They did not question the truthfulness of God's word. They agreed with God, however, they refused to fight for the land because they were fearful.

The Hebrew writer explains why they failed to enjoy the promise land. *So we see that they were not able to enter, because of their unbelief* (Heb 3:19). Their unbelief was manifested in fear—not actually disagreeing with God—but believing more in what they saw than in God who is unseen.

You see, many believers will agree on the promises of God, but when something bad happens to them, they will nevertheless fear even though God has promised to deliver them. Fear is a form of unbelief, and it will keep you from receiving from God.

How does fear work to keep you from receiving from God?

1. Fear will stop you from acting on the Word.

You must understand the true nature of faith. There are three essential ingredients that make up genuine faith: 1. Knowledge, 2. Agreement, and 3. Action. If one of these is missing, then there can not be real faith. You must know what God has promised, then you must agree with God, and finally, you must act on what you know.

There is a famous illustration that points out the futility of claiming to believe something when you do not want to commit yourself to it. A tight rope walker walked dangerously across one building to another, to the cheers of the spectators. He then walked across again pushing a wheelbarrow. Again the crowd cheered. Finally he yelled, "Who believes I can walk across to the other building with someone in the wheelbarrow?" There were no doubters. Everyone yelled, "Yeah, we believe you can do it!"

Then the performer asked, "Who will volunteer?" The audience was silent.

You see, for there to be real faith you must act on the Word. *So faith is dead without actions* (James 2:26, TCNT). *You see that his faith and his actions were working together, and his faith was made complete by what he did* (v. 22). Action *completes* faith. Without it your faith will only become mental assent. True faith must have actions.

For example, you may believe in tithing, but if you are afraid that you will not be able to pay your bills, you may end up robbing God of tithes and offerings. You still believe in it, but your actions prove otherwise. So fear can stop you from acting on the Word.

2. Fear will cause you to complain, grumble and cry out in fear.

The devil cannot stop God's promises from coming to pass in your life, so long as you continue to act on the Word and speak forth God's promises. But when you fail to confess the promises, and instead speak your fears, then the devil has control over your life.

The devil wants your tongue. If he can get your tongue, then, like a captain of a ship, he can guide your life because your tongue is like a rudder of a ship.

Please observe what God said to the grumbling spies: "*How long will this wicked community grumble against me? I have heard the complaints of these grum-*

bling Israelites. So tell them, 'As surely as I live, declares the LORD, I will do to you the very things I heard you say" (Num 14:27-28). God would judge them according to their *own* words. They declared that they would die in the desert, so God told them, "You are right, you will get what you said!"

The same thing occurs today. Even though God has declared exceeding, great and precious promises, you will ultimately get what you say about your life. If you say, "I'm going to lose my house", then you will lose it. If you say, "I'm dying," then you will die. If you say, "My marriage is over," then it is. You will get what you confess. Confession is possession. God wants you to receive what He has promised, but if you don't agree with Him, then you will not receive.

What made these spies speak such discouraging words? Fear. They feared the people more than God. When you fear God, you have nothing else to fear.

What is more real to you?

Faith is...the evidence of things not seen (Heb 11:1, KJV). *For we walk by faith, not by sight* (2 Cor 5:7-8, KJV). *So we fix our eyes not on what is seen, but on what is unseen. For what is seen is temporary, but what is unseen is eternal* (2 Cor 4:18). As you notice, walking by faith is the opposite of walking by sight. You cannot walk by faith and go by sight at the same time.

The term sight is a reference to our five senses. If you had to lose any of your five senses, I am sure sight would be the last one you would want to lose. The most important sense we have is sight. Sight is the primary of the five senses so it represents the senses. In reality, you cannot live by faith and go by your senses. Your senses may tell you one thing, and God may tell you something different. Let me show you the futility of walking by sight and yet trying to maintain faith in God.

Suppose a daughter was promised a dress by her mom, would the daughter look at her body to determine whether she has the dress? No, she looks at her mom who promised. She doesn't yell, "Mom, you promised me a dress, yet I am not wearing it."

The mom says, "Honey, I promised you the dress, so know I will get it for you. Be patient." The daughter would be foolish to look at herself to determine if the promise was true. The same is true with God. There is no use to look at your body, your bank account, or church to determine whether God has promised you the blessing. You look to Him and in due season you shall have it.

Suppose a tree was cut down. You will notice that the leaves are still green. That would not mean that the tree is alive. You know in time, the leaves will turn brown and fall off, never to return again. You do not look at the leaves to determine if the tree was alive. Similarly when God has spoken, the answer is there. God has cut off the works of the devil. You may still see fruits and evidence of the problem but you know in due time, it won't be there. God's word always prevails.

In the end, you have to determine what is more real to you: God's Word or the problems of life.

More with us than with them

There is a humorous story in the Bible which illustrates that God is more real than the natural world. The prophet Elisha was the number one enemy of the sinful king of Aram. He discovered Elisha was in the town of Dothan, so he sent a legion of troops to capture this one man. Secretly they surrounded the city at night. When Elisha's servant woke up, he was startled: "Oh, my lord, what shall we do?" (2 Kings 6:15)

With calmness, Elisha replied, "Don't be afraid, those who are with us are more than those who are with them." (2 Kings 6:16)

What! Are you kidding! This must have been what the servant thought! I can see him counting the enemies troops. After reaching seven thousand, he then pointed to his master and himself, "One, two." *Hmm, must be the new math!* Okay, maybe I am embellishing the story, but I think you get the point. It seemed foolish to think that there were more with those two than with the enemy. But it was the truth.

And Elisha prayed, "O LORD, open his eyes so he may see." Then the LORD opened the servant's eyes, and he looked and saw the hills full of horses and chariots of fire all around Elisha (2 Kings 6:17).

You see, there actually were more with them than with the enemy. They had angels protecting them. Of course, angels are ministering spirits and not flesh, and so without faith you don't accept them. Elisha, however, believed more in what he could not see than in what he could see. It was true that there was a strong force of soldiers there to capture Elisha, but it was equally true that there was a mighty, spiritual force of angels to fight for them — and fight they did. They blinded the troops and Elisha captured them instead.

The point of the story is clear, even when it is true that you have problems, it is equally true that God has given the answer. The question is, what will motivate you, the facts you see or the truth you cannot see? You must be moved by what you cannot see, because God is more real than natural reality. Yes, He created natural realities, but He also created spiritual realities, and the spiritual will always overrule the natural.

Always remember: God's promises overrule the problems. Angels always win over demons. Good always triumphs over evil. Light always dispels darkness. To live by faith means you side in with God and all the good He represents.

Step Seven:
CONFESS YOUR FAITH

The principle few Christians recognize is that their confession determines what they will receive. You do not receive what God "says" but what you "say." We saw this in the story of the ten spies who said, "We are going to die." God said, "That's right, you will get what you say." Even though God said the land was theirs, it was the spies' confession that determined what they were to possess.

God told Joshua, "I will give you every place where you set your foot, as I promised Moses" (Josh 1:3). Two important facts come forth from this statement. First, God promised Moses the land, but he failed to receive it. Second, Joshua would only receive God's promise if he set his foot on the land. Some have a strange and unbiblical understanding of God's sovereignty—they assume if God has promised them something, then it will automatically come true. Nothing could be farther from the truth.

God promises; but man must claim it. The way we claim under the New Covenant is by acting on the Word of God. The primary action is our confession.

Often when people hear the word "confession", they instinctively think of confessing sins. That is one side to confession and is brought out in James chapter 5 and 1 John chapter 1. However, the Bible teaches another neglected aspect of confession and that is the confession of faith.

Saying the Same Thing

Here is a passage that speaks on the confession of faith: *Therefore, since we have a great high priest who has gone through the heavens, Jesus the Son of God, let us hold firmly to the faith we profess* (Heb 4:14). The New King James says it this way, "*let us hold fast our confession.*"

The word confession is the Greek word *homologeo*. This word is a compilation of two words: *homo* which means the "same as" and *logeo* which means "to speak." Put them together and it means "to speak the same as" someone. In other words, confession always follows someone else's previous words. Confession is never an original word, but a repeat of what someone else has already said. In the biblical sense, confession is simply to agree with God and say the same thing He has spoken.

Many times people have thought that a person gets saved by confessing his sins, but this is not true. One gets saved by confessing *his faith*. Look at what Paul said about this: *But what does it say? "The word is near you; it is in your mouth and in your heart," that is, the word of faith we are proclaiming: That if you confess with your mouth, "Jesus is Lord," and believe in your heart that God raised him from the dead, you will be saved* (Rom 10:8-9).

You become saved by agreeing with God in your confession that Jesus was raised from the dead. You are simply confessing *the word that is near your mouth and heart.* Confession works when the Word of God is in your heart. When it is *real,* your confession of faith works to create the *reality* of it in your life.

This will not just work for salvation, but everything that is in the Word. In fact the word "saved" means complete health, soundness, and total blessings. It is like an "all-inclusive vacation package". In those deals everything is paid for—your hotel, food, travel, entertainment, etc. Well, God already thought of an all-inclusive salvation package. He paid for everything—your lodging in heaven, health in this life, and prosperity to enjoy your days on earth.

Paul had much more in mind than a ticket to heaven, as you will notice later. Romans verse 12: *For there is no difference between Jew and Gentile – the same Lord is Lord of all and richly blesses all who call on him.*

God does not save just in the sense of guaranteeing heaven at death, but He *richly blesses all* that confess the Word. You can receive everything God promised you as long as you maintain your confession of faith.

Your confession of faith should center on several important truths of the Word of God.

1. Redemption you have in Christ.

Redemption means to be purchased by God. We are not owned anymore by the devil. We are free. The Bible clearly teaches that we have already been redeemed. We are not looking for redemption, we have it now.

For he has rescued us from the dominion of darkness and brought us into the kingdom of the Son he loves, in whom we have redemption, the forgiveness of sins (Col 1:13-14).. I am not looking to be *rescued*; I am already rescued. I am already free from the dominion of Satan. I belong to God.

That must be your confession. Do not confess Satan's supremacy over your life. If you do, then you give him permission to dominate you.

Someone might say, "But Satan is ruling me." Maybe that is factual, but the confession of faith must be that you are ruling him. *Let the redeemed of the LORD say so* (Ps 107:2, KJV). You have to say it in order to establish it in your life.

You are also redeemed from the curse of the law: *Christ redeemed us from the curse of the law by becoming a curse for us, for it is written: "Cursed is everyone who is hung on a tree." He redeemed us in order that the blessing given to Abraham might come to the Gentiles through Christ Jesus, so that by faith we might receive the promise of the Spirit* (Gal 3:13-14).

The curse of the Law is outlined in detail in Deuteronomy chapter 28. There you will find an exhaustive list of curses for disobeying the law of God. They range from marital problems, to mental disorders, to physical sicknesses, and poverty. When you read the list, remember, you are redeemed from them. Praise God. Confess your redemption. Don't confess what you see, but what God already has said about you.

2. New Creation realities.

The Bible says, "*Therefore, if anyone is in Christ, he is a new creation; the old has gone, the new has come!*" (2 Cor 5:17) Many believers are beaten down by their past; they can't seem to get over it. The devil constantly reminds them of their past failures. What must you do if he does that to you? You must confess that the *old has gone*. You are a new creation.

Don't keep repeating your past mistakes, unless you share it as a testimony to help others. Forgive yourself. Confess that you are a new creation.

Paul goes on to say, "*God made him who had no sin to be sin for us, so that in him we might become the righteousness of God*" (v. 21).

Are you ready for this? You are so new that God declares you *the righteousness of God*. You are not simply forgiven, you are righteous. Wow!

"No, not me Pastor Brown, I could never be righteous!"

Yes, you are! Quit looking at the outward, see the inward man, you are righteous in God's sight. You do not *just* have right standing, you are as right as God can make a person. When you understand this, you will confess it until it becomes a reality to your spirit.

3. The indwelling of the Holy Spirit.

Too many believers are body conscious. Like many believers, you might be more aware of your outward condition than your inward condition. Inside of you dwells the Holy Spirit. He is not just a nice little influence you have, but He is the power of God. He is the One that raised Jesus from the dead — and He lives in you!

You cannot be defeated when you are mindful of the indwelling of the Holy Spirit. Some of the things I hear from Christians makes me wonder if they really know Who lives in them. They talk as if they are alone—no one is there to help them—when in reality, the Holy Spirit lives inside of them and would solve all their problems, but they don't confess Him. They confess loneliness instead of the Helper.

Paul also wondered if believers truly knew who lived in them: *Don't you know that you yourselves are God's temple and that God's Spirit lives in you?* (1 Cor 3:16) The fact that he uses a question to frame a spiritual truth shows that many believers *don't know that God's Spirit lives in* them. Many lack this revelation.

One way to build this revelation in you is by confessing it. Wake up in the morning and say, "I am God's temple and the Spirit of God lives in me!" You cannot have a bad day confessing this.

4. Christ present day ministry.

You have read the gospels. You know what Jesus taught and did while He was on the earth. But do you know what He is doing right now for you? Most shrug their shoulders, "I didn't know He was doing anything right now." He is. He is acting as high priest to God for you:

We do have such a high priest, who sat down at the right hand of the throne of the Majesty in heaven, and who serves in the sanctuary, the true tabernacle set up by the Lord, not by man (Heb 8:1-2). He serves us in three basic ways: 1. He intercedes for us; 2. He is the guarantee of the new covenant; 3. He is our advocate and mediator.

My heart is comforted knowing that my blessed Lord is praying for me. *Therefore he is able to save completely those who come to God through him, because he always lives to intercede for them* (Heb 7:25). Peter's heart must have leaped when Jesus told him, "I have prayed for you, Simon, that your faith may not fail" (Luke 22:32). I appreciate it when people tell me that they are praying for me, but nothing exhilarates my heart more than knowing that my high priest, Jesus Christ, is praying for me. Confess that He is praying for you.

Jesus has become the guarantee of a better covenant (Heb 7:22). Guarantees are meant to put your heart at ease, such as a manufacturer of an item you have purchase. They will fix anything you bought from them. We have great assurance in Christ. He will guarantee that we will receive every blessing under a better covenant. You do not need to worry whether your faith will work every time or not. Jesus will guarantee that you receive His promised blessings. You simply must maintain a good confession.

We are humans. Mistakes will occur, but praise God we have someone who will act as our advocate if we fall. *My dear children, I write this to you so that you will not sin. But if anybody does sin, we have one who speaks to the Father in our defense – Jesus Christ, the Righteous One* (1 John 2:1). Jesus will plead our case before the Supreme Court Justice of the Universe, and He is a better attorney than any "dream team" attorneys money can buy. You can be sure that you will be found "not guilty", not because you did not do wrong, but because Jesus' blood will cleanse you from sin. *He is the atoning sacrifice for our sins, and not only for ours but also for the sins of the whole world* (v. 2).

The only requirement to be forgiven is for you to confess your sin. Admit your mistakes. *If we confess our sins, he is faithful and just and will forgive us our sins and purify us from all unrighteousness* (1 John 1:9). Don't be concerned whether people will forgive you, so long as you have God's divine forgiveness.

Someone once said to a minister, "Oh, Reverend, I don't feel God has forgiven me. I have confessed my sins to God a hundred times."

The minister responded, "Well, I see your mistake. You have confessed it ninety-nine times too many." The minister went on to explain to the person that she cannot go by her feelings, but by the Word.

After you have confessed your sins, you must act like you are forgiven and do not act differently or shamefully. Don't be hesitant to do what God has told you to do. Don't let the past dictate your future. Act as if the Word is true. God has forgiven you, and so declare it.

I have seen too many ministers leave their calling over a blunder. Yes, the sin was awful, but nothing is so terrible that God will not forgive them. Consider Peter. He denied the Lord, not just once, but three times. This is possibly the worse sin any minister could ever commit. Yet Peter was forgiven and maintained his leadership among the disciples.

You, too, must go forward and confess your forgiveness, not just your sins over and over again. Claim you have an advocate before the Father.

Step Eight:
LOOK AT THE WORD, NOT YOUR PROBLEM

At this point, you may be thinking, "Why has God made it so difficult for me to receive? If he really wants to bless me, why doesn't He just do it? Why not just heal me now, or prosper me now? Why do I have to go through this thing called *faith*?"

I once had those same questions. I too had wondered why faith was so important to God. I was preparing what was meant to be an ordinary message on faith. While working on the sermon my curiosity about the importance of faith got to me. I knew there was more to this faith message than what I had understood. I am not the kind of person who is easily satisfied accepting something as true; I want to know *why* it is true. I wanted to know the answer to why faith was important. Why did God make faith the condition necessary to be saved or receive any blessing promised by God? Why faith, and not love. After all, didn't Paul say, *"And now these three remain: faith, hope and love. But the greatest of these is love"* (1 Cor 13:13)? If love was the greatest, then why was faith the requisite for salvation? Why not love. The Bible says: *For it is by grace you have been saved, through faith — and this not from yourselves, it is the gift of God – (Eph 2:8).*

Salvation is by grace *through faith.* Love, as important as it is, is not the requirement for salvation. Faith is! The Bible in fact says it is impossible to please God without faith: *And without faith it is impossible to please God, because anyone who comes to him must believe that he exists and that he rewards those who earnestly seek him* (Heb 11:6).

The Hebrew writer then gives the names of the faith hall of fame. Noah. Abraham. Moses. David. Elijah. The list goes on. All these people were different, none were perfect. When we look at the list for a common denominator, the writer wants us to realize that only one thread is woven through — and that was their faith. They were not necessarily kind, loving, or especially pure. Noah got drunk. Abraham and Isaac gave their wives away to other men. Still others brutally killed communities. David fell into adultery and plotted the murder of the husband. Elijah contemplated suicide. Despite their human frailties, God was pleased with them all. He was pleased because of one thing: they had faith. But why would that be pleasing? Let me explain why.

When the Bible says something *is impossible,* you better pay attention — especially when *it is impossible to please God without faith.* You may have every other good quality such as love, self-control, and joy, but without faith you still are not pleasing to God. You must find out why faith is so important to God.

God began to answer my deep yearning about faith and its importance. God showed me that in order to understand why faith was significant I had to understand the origin of sin.

The First Sin

Speculations abound concerning the nature of the original sin. Some see the sin as simply eating an apple. Others think it was sex. Still others elaborate on more fanciful ideas, imagining Adam and Eve committing high treason or some other contrived offense. The truth is clear: the sin of Adam and Eve is so obvious that we miss the real significance of the simple act of eating the forbidden fruit. Why was the fruit forbidden? Simply because God said so:

And the LORD God commanded the man, "You are free to eat from any tree in the garden; but you must not eat from the tree of the knowledge of good and evil, for when you eat of it you will surely die" (Gen 2:16-17).

There was nothing in the appearance of the fruit that gave any indication that the fruit was deadly, it looked harmless. As a matter of fact it looked good for food. However, if Adam and Eve believed God's Word that this fruit would kill them, then they would not have feasted on it. If they doubted God and chose to believe someone else's word, then they would have eaten it. Their decision to eat the fruit proved one thing: *they disbelieved the word of God.* The Original sin was doubt. Before they could even place the fruit in their mouths, they doubted that they would die. They believed they would grow wiser. And as Paul said, *"His eating is not from faith; and everything that does not come from faith is sin"* (Rom 14:23).

Do you understand the ramifications of doubt being the original sin? Since doubt was the original sin God had no choice but to require faith as mandatory for salvation. Faith reverses the effects of the original sin.

If the original sin was eating an apple, then not eating apples would reverse the original sin. If the sin was sex, then only abstinence could save us from sin. If the original sin was adultery, then only fidelity could save people. If the original sin was lying, then only telling the truth could save us. Do you understand? God, because of the nature of the original sin, had to make faith the cause of salvation. The original sin regulates the rules on how God could save humanity. Doubt was the problem, so faith is the solution.

So Adam and Eve doubted God, but why was that so deadly? Why did the fruit bring death? To understand how dreadful their sin was, you must understand the foundation and origin of the universe. How can you understand original sin if you don't understand the origin of the universe?

Origin of the Universe

Through faith we understand that the worlds were framed by the word of God, so that things which are seen were not made of things which do appear (Heb 11:3, KJV).

The worlds were framed by the word of God. A frame is the major support in a building. It is the structure on which the foundation is built. This verse is saying that the foundation and origin of the worlds is the word of God. God made everything by His Word.

Colossians 1:16 says: *For by him all things were created: things in heaven and on earth, visible and invisible, whether thrones or powers or rulers or authorities; all things were created by him and for him. He is before all things, and in him all things hold together.*

The word *him* is a reference to our Lord Jesus before His incarnation. *He is before all things.* Before there was anything, He existed, because He is the second person of the eternal God. He was the Word before He became a man.

John reaffirms this: *In the beginning was the Word, and the Word was with God, and the Word was God. He was with God in the beginning. Through him all things were made; without him nothing was made that has been made* (John 1:1-3).

Before Jesus was born in Bethlehem, He was the Word of God. It was the Word of God that made everything. This is why the first chapter in Genesis painstakingly emphasis the spoken word as the creative force of God. No less than nine times does Genesis chapter one say, "And God said … And God said … And God said!"

And God said, "Let there be light," and there was light. God saw that the light was good, and he separated the light from the darkness (Gen 1:3-4).

Notice the sequence: before God "saw" He first "said." That which is not seen made everything that is seen. In the language of the Bible, the *things which are seen were not made of things which do appear.* The invisible Word of God made everything that is visible. It even made the angels which are invisible. Nothing exists that does not owe its origin to the Word of God.

Not only did the Word of God make everything, the Word of God continues to *hold together* the worlds: *The Son is the radiance of God's glory and the exact representation of his being, sustaining all things by his powerful word* (Heb 1:3).

The Word of the Son of God continues to *sustain all things*. A building not only has a foundation, but it also has supports, such as beams, walls, and pillars. God's word is not just the foundation of the universe; it is also the current support and sustenance of the universe. Without the Word, the universe would presently collapse.

When you fully understand this, then you can appreciate how awful the original sin was. Adam and Eve disbelieved the Word of God, which is the source of everything. They abandoned the foundation and sustaining force of the universe. How could they continue to live when they removed themselves from the life support of the universe? This is why they died.

Man has Become Like One of Us

God's response to their disbelief seems awkward. Notice what God says: *And the LORD God said, "The man has now become like one of us, knowing good and evil. He must not be allowed to reach out his hand and take also from the tree of life and eat, and live forever"* (Gen 3:22).

Eating the tree of life would still give man life and eternity. What is the tree of life? *She is a tree of life to those who embrace her; those who lay hold of her will be blessed. By wisdom the LORD laid the earth's foundations, by understanding he set the heavens in place* (Prov 3:18-19).

This scripture teaches us that wisdom is the tree of life. Wisdom is the Greek word, *Logos*. You may recall this word in your study of the Bible, it is the word used for *Word of God*. We get our word logic from logos. Logic implies wisdom. Logos means the word and wisdom of God. Wisdom is personified as the tree of life, which is Jesus Christ. *He is the wisdom of God* (see 1 Cor 1:24).

The tree of life in the garden was the word of God. Do you see how Adam and Eve could have still eaten of the tree of life and escaped death? Death only came to them because they left the word of God, so if they would come back to the Word they would have lived. The Bible encourages us to eat from the tree of life, see Revelation 2:7 and 22:14.

Notice carefully what God said had happened to Adam: *"The man has now become like one of us."* The plural pronoun *us* refers to the Trinity: Father, Son and Holy Spirit. Please notice that God did *not* say, "Man has now become like us." Man never became like the Trinity. God did say, however, "The Man has now become like *one* of us." Not all three of us, but only "one" of us.

If there were three persons standing up and they said, "One of us shall be your friend," would you think all three would be your friends? No, because they said, "one" of us. One is singular. The Trinity was saying that man had become like one of the persons of the Trinity. Who of the three did man become like? That's simple: Who did man sin against? Man did not sin against the Father or the Holy Spirit. Thankfully, man did not sin against the Holy Spirit, or else there would have been no forgiveness, because whoever blasphemes the Spirit will never be forgiven.

Man had sinned against the Word by disbelieving the Word. The Word was his source of life, now man had chosen to live by another source — his own word. Man chose to live base on his own knowledge and wisdom. He left the Word in order to live by his own word. This is why God said, "Man had now become like one of us." Man had become like the Word in the sense that man would create his own existence based on his knowledge of good and evil. This is the current state of man.

Man lost his spiritual union with God, he became sense-ruled. The only knowledge he gets comes through the five senses. Whatever he sees and feels is what he believes. When Adam and Eve sinned, they left the spiritual realm and moved into the physical realm. *Then the eyes of both of them were opened, and they realized they were naked; so they sewed fig leaves together and made coverings for themselves* (Gen 3:7).

Prior to the fall, they were so spiritually minded that they had not noticed they were naked, but once they left faith in the Word, they became concerned over what they saw. Their eyes became the source of what was real. Their sight now governed them. It was also their sight that caused them to fall: *When the woman saw that the fruit of the tree was good for food and pleasing to the eye, and also desirable for gaining wisdom, she took some and ate it. She also gave some to her husband, who was with her, and he ate it* (Gen 3:6).

She *saw that the fruit was good for food.* Her eyes fooled her. She believed more in what she saw than what God had said. God said the fruit was deadly, but she saw that it was good. She went by her sight, and left the faith that was in the word of God. She thought she would get wisdom, but instead she got death. You've heard the saying, "What you see is what you get!" This was not true for Eve. What she saw was not what she got.

God had a plan to redeem man. Since man had disbelieved the Word and thus replaced the Word with himself, God knew the only redemption would be to get man to believe in the Word again. But how was God going to do that? Man can only believe in what he sees.

"That is it!" God exclaimed. Since man had become like the Word, the Word would have to become like the man. The incarnation was the solution to get man to believe in the Word again. *The Word became flesh and made his dwelling among us. We have seen his glory, the glory of the One and Only, who came from the Father, full of grace and truth* (John 1:14).

The only way for man to believe in the Word is he must *see his glory*. God must become flesh so man could believe. God must enter the world of man.

That which was from the beginning, which we have heard, which we have seen with our eyes, which we have looked at and our hands have touched — this we proclaim concerning the Word of life. The life appeared; we have seen it and testify to it, and we proclaim to you the eternal life, which was with the Father and has appeared to us (1 John 1:1-2).

Have you noticed the prominence of the senses? *We have heard…we have looked at and our hands*

have touched ...The life appeared; we have seen it.
Unless man could touch the Word with his senses,
he could not believe. So the Word had to become
flesh.

Listen, when someone believes in Christ, they
actually believe in the Word, which made everything. To believe in Christ is to reverse the sin of
Adam and Eve. They disbelieved the Word, so the
Word became flesh for us to believe. Faith is within everyone's grasps. Everyone can believe in what
they see. Christ has come, the apostles are witnesses of what they saw, and now we believe in their
testimony, which is the testimony of their senses.
They saw the resurrection and have told us so; we
either choose to believe in their testimony or dis-
believe their testimony.

Once we believe their testimony, we leave the
realm of the senses, and enter the realm of the
Spirit. God did not intend for us to live by our
senses. Christ entered the sense realm once, then
when we believe in Him, God gives us the Spirit so
that we can live by faith again. Faith brings us back
to our original state.

Thomas's Faith

Our faith is not based on our senses, but based
on what God has said in His Word. God told
Thomas, *"Because you have seen me, you have
believed; blessed are those who have not seen and yet
have believed"* (John 20:29).

God could have left Jesus on the earth for all to
see Him, multitudes would have touched His
wounds and believed. That would have made our

senses the basis of faith. God did not want us to live by what we see. *We live by faith, not by sight* (2 Cor 5:7).

Instead, God received Jesus into heaven, out from our sight, so that we would be forced to live by faith again. Jesus said, "*I tell you the truth: It is for your good that I am going away*" (John 16:7). If Jesus had stayed, then none of us would be living by faith. Jesus continued, "*Unless I go away, the Counselor will not come to you; but if I go, I will send him to you*" (John 16:7). Receiving Christ was our first act of faith as a sinner; however, receiving the Holy Spirit is our first act of faith as a child of God.

Many believers falter at this point. It becomes too difficult to receive the Spirit, because the believer is unwilling to leave the realm of the senses and receive an invisible Spirit. Christ is physical; He has a body; He walked on the earth. It is easy to receive a person like this, but on the other hand, the Spirit does not have a body, He has never been seen, so it becomes difficult for many Christians to receive the Spirit, but you can if you are willing to live by faith.

Look carefully at what Jesus said about the Spirit: "*And I will ask the Father, and he will give you another Counselor to be with you forever — the Spirit of truth. The world cannot accept him, because it neither sees him nor knows him. But you know him, for he lives with you and will be in you*" (John 14:16-17).

Notice that *the world cannot accept him, because it neither sees him nor knows him.* The world cannot accept the Holy Spirit because it cannot see Him. The word *world* speaks of unsaved people. They have not made their first faith decision to accept

Christ who was seen; so how can they be expected to make a more difficult faith decision to accept the Holy Spirit who has never been seen.

As a believer, your act of faith is to accept the Holy Spirit. If you can't accept the Holy Spirit, then how will you be able to accept any other promises given by God?

As Saint Paul writes: *We have not received the spirit of the world but the Spirit who is from God, that we may understand what God has freely given us...The man without the Spirit does not accept the things that come from the Spirit of God, for they are foolishness to him, and he cannot understand them, because they are spiritually discerned* (1 Cor 2:12 and 14).

Many Christians consider such promises of divine healing, speaking in tongues, exorcism, and the gifts of the Spirit as foolish. Why do they consider those things foolish? They do so because they have not received the Spirit. As we receive the Spirit, we begin to live in the Spirit, not in the flesh or fleshly realm. We live not by what we see, feel, or hear, we live by the teaching of the Spirit. He opens the word of God to us, and we begin to learn all the things that God has freely given us. And when problems come in our lives, the Holy Spirit whispers to our hearts to remind us not to look at our problems, but to look at the Word.

Step Nine:
DON'T MISUNDERSTAND GOD

L et's look closely at the original sin: *Now the serpent was more crafty than any of the wild animals the LORD God had made. He said to the woman, "Did God really say, 'You must not eat from any tree in the garden'?" The woman said to the serpent, "We may eat fruit from the trees in the garden, but God did say, 'You must not eat fruit from the tree that is in the middle of the garden, and you must not touch it, or you will die.'" "You will not surely die," the serpent said to the woman. "For God knows that when you eat of it your eyes will be opened, and you will be like God, knowing good and evil." When the woman saw that the fruit of the tree was good for food and pleasing to the eye, and also desirable for gaining wisdom, she took some and ate it. She also gave some to her husband, who was with her, and he ate it. Then the eyes of both of them were opened, and they realized they were naked; so they sewed fig leaves together and made coverings for themselves* (Gen 3:1-7).

The first words to fall from the lips of the serpent were, *"Did God really say?"* The issue around the first sin involves the veracity of the Word of God. Can God be trusted? Is His word reliable? Will God lie? The serpent, which we know was

Satan, attempted to inject doubt in the mind of Eve concerning the reliability of the word of God. He does not begin by attacking directly the truthfulness of God; instead, he starts off by misquoting God. *"Did God really say, 'You must not eat from any tree in the garden'?"* There was only *one tree* they could not eat; yet Satan makes it appear *that any tree in the garden* was off limits.

The woman counters, *"We may eat fruit from the trees in the garden, but God did say, 'You must not eat fruit from the tree that is in the middle of the garden, and you must not touch it, or you will die.'"* Now here we find a very subtle, almost, imperceptible error on the part of the woman. She incorrectly quotes the Word of God. Doubt does not begin by disagreeing with God, but by misunderstanding God. God said nothing about *touching* the fruit; only that they could not *eat of it*.

There was something else she said, which was incorrect. She was not precise in quoting God. There were two trees in the *middle of the garden*. One was the tree of life and the other the tree of the knowledge of good and evil. There was no ban on the tree of life; they were free to eat of that fruit. However, in Eve's mind, she felt she had better stay away from any tree in the middle of the garden. She said, *"You must not eat fruit from the tree that is in the middle of the garden."* Which tree? Her words show that she did not understand God's command. She should have said, *"You must not eat fruit from the tree of the knowledge of good and evil."*

Do not think I am being technical. This is where doubt creeps into our lives. Unless you precisely know what God has said, you are likely to fall into the same error as Eve. It is not simply "hearing" the Word which is important but "understanding" it.

Parable of the Sower

Jesus emphasized this point in His most important parable: *"When anyone hears the message about the kingdom and does not understand it, the evil one comes and snatches away what was sown in his heart"* (Matt 13:19). How can the devil *snatch away* the Word? The devil easily stole the Word because the person who heard it did *not understand it.*

The Hebrew writer plays on this concept of understanding. Let's first look at chapter 11:1, *"Now faith is the substance of things hoped for, the evidence of things not seen"* (KJV). The Greek word for "substance" is *hupostasis.* The word is formed by two Greek words, *hupo* which means "sub", hence the word for *sub*stance. The other Greek word is *stasis* which means "stance". So the King James transliterated it as "substance" or "to stand under." It speaks of a foundation. A foundation is something that you can stand on.

Now notice later the Hebrew writer plays word games with this expression. *"Through faith we understand that the worlds were framed by the word of God"* (v. 3, KJV). What framed the worlds? The Word of God framed it. But the Hebrew writer does *not* say we "believe" the worlds were framed by the Word, but he does say we *"understand"* the worlds were framed by the Word.

Reverse the word "under-stand" and it comes out "stand-under." Do you get it? We can stand on the Word of God when we understand it. Wow!

You cannot really stand on the Word of God when you do not understand what God has really said. This was Eve's problem. She was not defiantly rebelling against God, but she was deceived because she failed to truly understand what God said. *Eve was deceived by the serpent's cunning* (2 Cor 11:2). So doubt can really be a product of misunderstandings.

Consider a boss who gives an instruction to his employee. If the employee misunderstands the boss, then she will likely appear to have disobeyed him. The disobedience is real, but based on misunderstandings. All mistakes are a result of misunderstandings. This happens all the time in human relations; this is what happened with Eve, she did disobeyed God, but she did it because she did not understand what God had actually said.

I see many sincere believers struggling to receive everything God has for them, because they have been deceived through misunderstandings, consequently they fail to receive. In the next, and last chapter, I want to explain what God has really given to us in Christ, so that there will be no misunderstandings.

Step Ten:
CLAIM ALL GOD'S PROMISES

But as surely as God is faithful, our message to you is not "Yes" and "No." For the Son of God, Jesus Christ, who was preached among you by me and Silas and Timothy, was not "Yes" and "No," but in him it has always been "Yes." *For no matter how many promises God has made, they are "Yes" in Christ. And so through him the "Amen" is spoken by us to the glory of God* (2 Cor 1:18-20).

The Apostles preached a complete gospel filled with healing and miracles. Yet, I hear debates about whether tongues, healing, prosperity or exorcisms are really promises of God.

Some will say, "That promise belongs to the Old Covenant, and this other one belongs to the Millennium, and when the Tribulation begins, God will start to fulfill this distinct promise, and concerning the promises to do miracles, those belonged to the Early Church." You see, all that rationale is simply doubt and unbelief pretending to be sound doctrine. The Apostles clearly differentiated themselves from those who preached a *"Yes" and "No"* message. Paul says, *"For no matter how many promises God has made, they are "Yes" in Christ."* Those words settle the issue quite forthrightly. I am obligated to believe in every promise of God.

1. God promises the Spirit.

For example, many question the promise of the Holy Spirit. They do not think the Spirit is for them. Many churches ban any manifestations of the Spirit, even though Paul said, "*Do not forbid speaking in tongues*" (1 Cor 14:39) churches ignore this command and ban tongues anyway. Why? They do so because they do not think we can receive the Spirit in the same way as the early church. They erroneously think the tongues in the Bible are a different kind of tongues spoken by modern day Pentecostals. Let me show you that this gift was to continue down through all generations. Look at what Peter said.

"*Repent and be baptized, every one of you, in the name of Jesus Christ for the forgiveness of your sins. And you will receive the gift of the Holy Spirit. The promise is for you and your children and for all who are far off – for all whom the Lord our God will call*" (Acts 2:38-39). Who is this promise for? *For all whom the Lord our God will call*. Not just for the early church, but for all.

And how did the church receive the Spirit? *When the day of Pentecost came, they were all together in one place. Suddenly a sound like the blowing of a violent wind came from heaven and filled the whole house where they were sitting. They saw what seemed to be tongues of fire that separated and came to rest on each of them. All of them were filled with the Holy Spirit and began to speak in other tongues as the Spirit enabled them* (Acts 2:1-4).

"But Pastor Brown, our church does not believe in speaking in tongues."

I realize many churches do not, but why? May I tell you the real reason why many churches do not accept tongues? They do not accept tongues because of unbelief; they doubt the reality of tongues. Oh, they try their best to explain it away, but in the end, it is simply unbelief in the word of God. There is nothing remotely in the Bible or in church history that remotely proves tongues were to disappear. This gift is for *you and your children and for all who are far off*. Even Gentiles were to receive this gift, yet many think this gift was for the Jews only. This is not what Peter preached. It is for *all whom the Lord our God will call.*

"But what about 1 Corinthian chapter 13? Didn't Paul say that tongues were to disappear?"

The passage is as follows: *Love never fails. But where there are prophecies, they will cease; where there are tongues, they will be stilled; where there is knowledge, it will pass away. For we know in part and we prophesy in part, but when perfection comes, the imperfect disappears* (1 Cor 13:8-10).

The argument goes something like this: "The *perfection* in this scripture refers to the completion of the Bible. And since the Bible is already here with us, speaking in tongues and prophecy should stop."

This interpretation is completely wrong. Paul could not have referred to the completion of the Scriptures as the *perfection* in 1 Corinthians 13, simply because Paul said in 1 Corinthians 1:7, *Therefore you do not lack **any spiritual gift** as you eagerly wait for our Lord Jesus Christ to be revealed.* Paul believed that all the spiritual gifts would remain until Jesus Christ comes back.

In 1 Corinthians 13 Paul was referring to the Second Coming as the *perfection*. When Christ comes back there won't be anymore sickness, thus no need for the gifts of healing. There won't be any confusion, thus no need for the word of wisdom. There won't be any evil spirits, thus no need for the discerning of spirits. I think you can see that the *perfection* is referring to the *perfect age* that Christ' Second Coming will bring.

There are no scriptural reasons for doubting the validity of tongues or any of the gifts of the Spirit. The only reason people doubt the gifts of the Spirit is they *do not combine* their scripture reading *with faith*.

2. God promises health.

The same doubt permeates the modern church when it comes to divine healing. How rare it is to see the average church praying over the sick. Yes, they go to hospitals and pray that God will give them patience, but when God does heal, people are surprised. Apologists and ministers spend countless hours criticizing those with a healing ministry. Instead, they should repent for their unbelief in God's healing power.

"Oh, pastor, I believe in God's healing power. I am just skeptical of those who claim to be able to heal."

Wouldn't it be nice if God healed according to your way? He would sovereignly and without the aid of men, heal the sick. However, God has chosen to heal through people. *And in the church God has appointed...workers of miracles, also those having gifts of healing* (1 Cor 12:28).

Many argue with God's appointments. You are not the senate, however; God does not ask you to confirm His appointments. He appoints *workers of miracles* and *those having gifts of healing*, with or without your approval.

You see the root of unbelief regarding divine healing and miracles stems from the fact that our eyes are on the vessel instead of being on the Lord. This was the problem in Nazareth.

Coming to his hometown, he began teaching the people in their synagogue, and they were amazed. "Where did this man get this wisdom and these miraculous powers?" they asked. "Isn't this the carpenter's son? Isn't his mother's name Mary, and aren't his brothers James, Joseph, Simon and Judas? Aren't all his sisters with us? Where then did this man get all these things?" And they took offense at him. But Jesus said to them, "Only in his hometown and in his own house is a prophet without honor." And he did not do many miracles there because of their lack of faith (Matt 13:54-58).

It would have been far more convenient if the Messiah was not human or if He had not had a family. Today, we would love it for God to bypass the anointed vessel and simply heal on His own. But God does not work that way, He works through people.

When Benny Hinn heals, many become skeptical because their eyes are on his wavy hair or deep middle-eastern accent or on his bright, white suits. Their eyes are deceiving them. Do not look on the outward appearance, but look to the anointing.

"Don't misunderstand me, pastor, I believe people are truly healed. But what about the ones who do not get well? We must assure them that God has a plan for them also."

Yes, he does, His plan is to heal them. Just because they did not receive their healing at Benny Hinn's meeting or immediately after praying for healing does not mean they will not get healed. God wants them healed, too. But sometimes God prefers to heal apart from the healing ministry. Nevertheless, He wants everyone healed.

Now, this is where doubt creeps in again. Many believe in God's healing power, but they doubt that healing is for all. Remember, James said, "*God gives to all.*" God is not a respecter of persons. He respects faith. Some have been taught to pray like this: "God, if it is your will, heal me, but if not let me have the grace to bear it." Sounds spiritual, but it is not. There is no faith in that prayer. The person who prays like that is not confident of recovering. Faith cannot exist where the will of God is not known. Faith must know God's will. Only one person in the New Testament prayed a prayer similar to this: *A man with leprosy came and knelt before him and said, "Lord, if you are willing, you can make me clean." Jesus reached out his hand and touched the man. "I am willing," he said. "Be clean!" Immediately he was cured of his leprosy* (Matt 8:2-3).

This is the only man with a theology of doubt who got healed. He was not sure of the Lord's willingness to heal, so he prayed, "*Lord, if you are willing, you can make me clean.*" However, Jesus did not allow the man to be unsure of His willingness to heal, so Jesus said, *"I am willing."* Jesus had to remove the man's doubt before He could heal him. The Lord will have to do the same for you. Before He can heal you, your doubt concerning God's willingness to heal you must be gone.

I know of only one way to know for sure that God wants me healed, and that is if I know He wants *everyone* healed. Everyone includes me. Jesus revealed the will of God to us by healing everyone who came to Him with faith. Look at the following scriptures:

When the sun was setting, the people brought to Jesus all who had various kinds of sickness, and laying his hands on each one, he healed them (Luke 4:40).

Jesus went throughout Galilee, teaching in their synagogues, preaching the good news of the kingdom, and healing every disease and sickness among the people (Matt 4:23).

When evening came, many who were demon-possessed were brought to him, and he drove out the spirits with a word and healed all the sick (Matt 8:16).

Jesus went through all the towns and villages, teaching in their synagogues, preaching the good news of the kingdom and healing every disease and sickness (Matt 9:35).

Jesus said, *"For I have come down from heaven not to do my will but to do the will of him who sent me"* (John 6:38). Jesus' actions were the will of God. Since He healed everyone without exception, we know it is God's will to heal everyone.

Let me illustrate why it is so important to believe that God wants to heal everyone. Suppose you were in a meeting with a hundred people, and a man stood up and said, "Ladies and Gentlemen,

I am so rich that I have the ability to give everyone a thousand dollars." Would you have reason to believe you were going to be a thousand dollars richer? Not really, because the man's ability says nothing of his willingness.

Again, suppose he said, "I am going to give five people a thousand dollars." You still would not believe for sure that you would get a thousand dollars, because the odds are against you.

Let's take this analogy further: Suppose he said he is going to give everyone but one person a thousand dollars. Now, at this point, your faith is stronger. You have a very good reason to believe that you will receive a thousand dollars; however, there is a slight possibility that you might be the one exception.

You see, unless the man promised everyone a thousand dollars, you could not be totally confident of receiving the money. Once the promise is made to everyone then you may be sure you will receive a thousand dollars.

Evangelicals have no difficulty in believing that salvation is for all. When a person comes forward to accept Christ, the minister is bold to say: "You are forgiven." But when a sick person comes forward, they lose their boldness to say, "You are healed by the stripes of Jesus." Why?

Jesus gave the reason in Luke 5:20-23: *When Jesus saw their faith, he said, "Friend, your sins are forgiven." The Pharisees and the teachers of the law began thinking to themselves, "Who is this fellow who speaks blasphemy? Who can forgive sins but God alone?" Jesus knew what they were thinking and asked, "Why are you thinking these things in your hearts? Which is easier: to say, 'Your sins are forgiven,' or to say, 'Get up and walk'?*

It is much *easier to say,* "Your sins are forgiven," than to say to a cripple, "Get up and walk." It is always harder to believe for healing than salvation. Since it takes greater faith to believe for healing, how can we expect to have faith for healing if we doubt that healing is for all? The only reason evangelicals shy away when it comes to healing is simply because it is harder to believe for healing than it is for salvation. The answer to doubt is not to compromise the gospel message of healing, but rather to preach healing with more boldness and faith. Until we are sure that healing is for all, there will always be an element of uncertainty.

3. God promises wealth.

The subject of prosperity is tied directly with tithing. They are almost used synonymously. The reason is clear, God promises to bless those that tithe. *Bring the whole tithe into the storehouse, that there may be food in my house. Test me in this," says the LORD Almighty, "and see if I will not throw open the floodgates of heaven and pour out so much blessing that you will not have room enough for it"* (Mal 3:10).

The main argument is whether tithing is New Testament or simply an Old Testament law. If it belongs exclusively to the Old Testament, then the promise to open the windows of heaven also belongs only to the Jews. If the later argument is right then this promise of prosperity is excluded, however Paul said, *"For no matter how many prom-*

ises God has made, they are "Yes" in Christ." This issue is not simply arguing against tithing but arguing against the "promise of God" to open the windows of heaven and to pour our all sorts of blessings, including finances.

This issue is important for both the individual claim of prosperity and the churches claim for prosperity. For you see, if a church does not believe in tithing, they will not only hinder God's people from prospering but hinder the church as well. So let me explain why I believe tithing is for the Christian and is the right of the ministry to receive it.

An important thing to remember is this: tithing began before the law was introduced. The Law simply regulated the tithe. Abraham tithed to Melchizedek four hundred years before the time of Moses and the Law, and according to Romans 4:12 we are to walk in the footsteps of the faith of Abraham. If tithing was good for him, it should be good for us, too.

We give tithes like Abraham gave them—not by the Law but by faith. And beside that, if the people of God paid ten percent before the Law and ten percent under the Law, should we, who live by grace, be doing any less when we have a better covenant (Heb 7:22)?

There is a passage in Hebrews which deals with this issue directly. It is Hebrews 7:8: *In the one case, the tenth is collected by men who die; but in the other case, by him who is declared to be living.* Melchizedek received Abraham's tithe. The Hebrew writer shows that Melchizedek is a prefigure of Christ. We can conclude that just as

Abraham gave a tithe to Melchizedek we give a tithe to Christ who is declared to be living.

Some people think this is a new issue. It is as old as the second century when more and more Gentiles were being converted. The early Jewish believers had no problem with tithing since they had done it under the Law and gave it to the priests. They simply gave their tithe to the elders of the church and did it by love. However, as the church became less Jewish this issue came up to the church fathers. They answered the question of tithing with Matthew 23:23: *"Woe to you, teachers of the law and Pharisees, you hypocrites! You give a tenth of your spices — mint, dill and cummin. But you have neglected the more important matters of the law — justice, mercy and faithfulness. You should have practiced the latter, without neglecting the former."*

Notice Jesus said, *"You should have practiced the latter (justice, mercy and faithfulness), without neglecting the former (tithing)."* The fathers argued, and rightfully so, that Jesus' word ends the discussion. Since Jesus said not to neglect the former — being tithing — then no believer should neglect tithing. I wholeheartedly agree!

Paul also uses the pattern of tithing under the law in 1 Corinthians 9:13-14 and says, *"Don't you know that those who work in the temple get their food from the temple, and those who serve at the altar share in what is offered on the altar? In the same way, the Lord has commanded that those who preach the gospel should receive their living from the gospel."* Paul argues that just as the priests got their food from the tithes of the people, so the preachers should live the *same way*. This passage clearly shows the mentality of the apostle and his understanding of carrying over the concept of tithing into the church.

The passage that is often used to contradict this is 2 Corinthians 9:7: *Each man should give what he has decided in his heart to give, not reluctantly or under compulsion, for God loves a cheerful giver.* The argument goes something like this: "Each believer has a right to decide for himself what to give and should not be told what percentage he should contribute."

The problem with this argument is that the above passage is not dealing with giving to support the church, but rather giving to the poor. Under the Law, giving to the poor was a freewill offering. The Law commanded freewill offerings as well as tithes:

*But you are to seek the place the LORD your God will choose from among all your tribes to put his Name there for his dwelling. To that place you must go; there bring your burnt offerings and sacrifices, your **tithes** and special gifts, what you have vowed to give and your **freewill offerings**, and the firstborn of your herds and flocks* (Deut 12:5-6).

It is quite inconsistent for anti-tithing preachers to appeal to freewill offerings yet claim that tithing has been abolished. Both tithing and freewill offerings were incorporated in the Law as the above passage shows, because they preceded the Law, thus they both should be practiced. The burden of proof is placed on those who teach that tithing has been abolished. If so, where in the New Testament does it clearly say that tithing has been abolished? It doesn't.

One last thing, notice the resemblance of the language Paul uses in the passage in Galatians and compare it with the Old Testament passage about tithing: *Anyone who receives instruction in the word must share **all good things** with his instructor* (Gal 6:6). The Old Testament passage says, *And you and the Levites and the aliens among you shall rejoice in **all the good things** the LORD your God has given to you and your household. When you have finished setting aside a tenth of all your produce in the third year, the year of the tithe, you shall give it to the Levite, the alien, the fatherless and the widow, so that they may eat in your towns and be satisfied* (Deut 26:11-12).

Galatians 6 is dealing with giving to the teachers of the gospel and he uses the same language about the Levites receiving the tithe of the people and he calls it "*all good things*". This is pretty good internal evidence that the early church tithed to the ministers of the gospel; although, I admit it is not explicit evidence.

However, I gave plenty of other scriptural proof that tithing was practiced by the early church and it should be practiced by us. The good news is that God will bless you with prosperity if you tithe.

4. God promises deliverance.

The national media has sought me out because of the ministry of deliverance. My ministry of deliverance has appeared on MSNBC and the History Channel. One news organization, KTLA from Los Angeles traveled across two states to do a three minute news story. I asked them, "Why did you travel almost 800 miles to come here, why not just pick a church in your area and do a story on deliverance?"

They responded, "No one in our area is approachable to do this openly." This does not mean that churches do not believe in deliverance, but they have not made it an important area of ministry. This is an indication to the lack of understanding people have regarding deliverance. Jesus was open to the ministry of deliverance. *That evening after sunset the people brought to Jesus all the sick and demon-possessed. The whole town gathered at the door, and Jesus healed many who had various diseases. He also drove out many demons* (Mark 1:32-34).

Jesus' supernatural ministry consisted of two basic things: He healed all the sick and drove out many demons, not just a few demons, but many. The Church has started to rise up in the healing ministry, but they are far behind in the ministry of deliverance. Yet, Jesus gave us those two main abilities when we preach the gospel. Look what He told us: *And these signs will accompany those who believe: In my name they will drive out demons; they will speak in new tongues; they will pick up snakes with their hands; and when they drink deadly poison, it will not hurt them at all; they will place their hands on sick people, and they will get well"* (Mark 16:17-18).

The first sign on the list is driving out demons, yet that seems to be last on people's list. This should not be.

One religious dogma that has become a sacred cow which people hold to that keeps them from exercising dominion over demons is the false idea that Christians cannot have demons, so they argue that Jesus gave the disciples power to drive out demons only from sinners. Assuming that they are right, then why don't they drive them out of sinners? The critics of the deliverance ministry seem to complain about anyone driving out demons, yet they do not lift a finger to show how it is done. Before they complain about the technique people have used to drive out demons, they better be prepared to show how it is really done.

Those who teach that Christians cannot have demons and that only sinners need deliverance put themselves in a "Catch 22" situation. While they advocate a deliverance ministry, they always find an exception to actually exorcise this power. Here's what I mean. They lecture that deliverance is for the sinner, however, they will not actually drive out demons from them, because they will convince themselves, "It is pointless to drive out demons from sinners, because they still belong to Satan. What we must do is bring them to Christ." So when they bring them to Christ, they argue, "Now since they are a Christians, they cannot have demons anymore." In the end, they do not attempt to drive out demons while they were sinners, and now they excuse themselves from doing it because the sinners are now Christians. So no matter what they say, they always find a rule to exempt themselves from deliverance, and then they condemn those who obey the Great Commission.

I believe that both sinners and saints may be bothered by demons. For sure, Christians will not be possessed in their spirits by demons, because their spirits are new creatures, however, their bodies await the resurrection of the dead and their minds are still being worked on in renewal. The body and mind may still be oppressed and may be the habitation of demons. Those believers who have either yielded to demons or ignorantly allowed demons to infiltrate their lives may need deliverance. Of course, many sinners will need deliverance as well, often when they come to get saved. I have successfully driven out demons from Christians and non-Christians alike.

It is not difficult to drive out demons. You drive them out by ordering them to go. You do not need a prayer book, beads, holy water, blessed oil or anything else except faith in the Word of God. Simply use your authority in the name of Jesus. Jesus said, *"In my name they will drive out demons."* The secret is the use of the name. When you speak in the name of Jesus, you are speaking in His authority, not your own. You know that demons must listen to you because you belong to Christ and are following His command.

I do not depend on my merits to drive out demons. I do not think they will listen to me because I am nationally known as the "Exorcist." No, they will listen to me solely because Christ has victory over them, and His victory becomes my victory. I depend totally on Christ's value and not my worth.

You need to learn to accept the fact that you can drive out demons because Christ is there with you to drive them out. You do not need to worry that your life is not perfect or that there is some hidden sin in your life that will cause the devil to refuse to go. If you are thinking about that, then your mind is on your righteousness and not Christ.

The story of the Lion King comes to my mind. Little Simba got himself into trouble by going outside the boundaries of his father's kingdom. *Sounds familiar?* There he ran into some mean, hungry hyenas. His life was about to be snatched, when he decided out of desperation to let out a roar. Of course, being a cub, his roar was pathetic. He sounded like a pussy cat instead, however, this time, when he let out a roar; an earth-shaking, terrible roar was heard. The hyenas ran in fear. A smile broke across Simba's face for he thought they were frightened of him, but behind him stood his bulky father, Mufasa. The roar was really the roar of his dad.

When I first saw that scene, the Holy Spirit spoke to me, "You see, that is God's people. When they speak in the Name of Jesus, the devil hears the roar of the Son of God." Praise the Lord!

You see, when you depend on the name and authority of Christ, the devil does not hear some measly, pitiful order to go, but he hears the voice of the Son of God.

For a complete list of books, tapes,
CDs, videos, and DVDs,

Contact:

TOM BROWN MINISTRIES
PO Box 27275
El Paso, Texas 79926
USA

Phone (915) 857-0962
Internet: www.tbm.org
Email: tom@tbm.org